D0172312

Multicultural Mathematics

DAVID NELSON is Lecturer in Education at the University of Manchester. His recent publications include *The Penguin Dictionary of Mathematics* and *Extensions of Calculus*, published by Cambridge University Press.

GEORGE GHEVERGHESE JOSEPH is Senior Lecturer in Economic and Social Statistics at the University of Manchester. His recent publications include *The Crest of the Peacock: Non-European Roots of Mathematics*, published by I. B. Tauris and Penguin.

JULIAN WILLIAMS is Senior Lecturer in Education and Director of the Mechanics in Action Project at the University of Manchester. His recent publications include *Practical Projects with Mathematics* and *Mechanics in Action*, both published by Cambridge University Press.

Multicultural Mathematics

David Nelson, George Gheverghese Joseph, and Julian Williams

Oxford   New York
OXFORD UNIVERSITY PRESS

Oxford University Press, Walton Street, Oxford OX2 6DP

Oxford New York
Athens Auckland Bangkok Bombay
Calcutta Cape Town Dar es Salaam Delhi
Florence Hong Kong Istanbul Karachi
Kuala Lumpur Madras Madrid Melbourne
Mexico City Nairobi Paris Singapore
Taipei Tokyo Toronto
and associated companies in
Berlin Ibadan

Oxford is a trade mark of Oxford University Press

© David Nelson, George Gheverghese Joseph, and Julian Williams 1993

First published 1993 as an Oxford University Press paperback

British Library Cataloguing in Publication Data
Data available

Library of Congress Cataloging in Publication Data
Nelson, David.
Multicultural mathematics / David Nelson, George Gheverghese Joseph,
and Julian Williams.
p. cm. Includes bibliographical references.
1. Mathematics—Study and teaching. 2. Intercultural education.
I. Joseph, George Gheverghese. II. Williams, Julian. III. Title.
510'.71—dc20 QA11.N43 1993 92-17031
ISBN 0-19-282241-1

10 9 8 7 6 5

Printed in Great Britain by
Biddles Ltd
Guildford and King's Lynn

Preface

'THIS were a wikked way · but who-so hadde a gyde
That wolde folwen vs eche a fote;' · þus þis folke hem mened.

William Langland, *Piers the Plowman*, Passus VI*

This book is about the teaching of mathematics from a multicultural or global perspective.

Its origins go back to Joseph's 1984 article in the *Times Educational Supplement*. Williams and Nelson, who were training teachers and giving advanced courses in mathematics education in the same university as Joseph, contacted him, and a partnership emerged called Elementary Mathematics from a Multicultural Standpoint (EMMS). A spate of in-service and extramural courses for teachers, parents, and administrators followed, and, with the support of PGCE students, some teaching materials were developed and tried in Manchester schools. In 1987 a useful link was made with the M:ATH group in Paris (Mathématiques: Approche par des Textes Historiques).

These activities met with an encouraging response from teachers and pupils, but a repeated call (encapsulated in the quotation above) was for something more substantial; a book or books which set out our position, provided extensive sources of information, and discussed possibilities for the classroom.

Thus the EMMS team has been preoccupied recently with two books: *The Crest of the Peacock* (1991), in which Joseph makes an extensive survey of the development of mathematics in non-European cultures, and the present title, edited by Nelson.

* 'A wild way were this, save a guide were at hand,
To follow us each foot' so the folks complained.

Piers the Plowman, trans. W. W. Skeat
(London: Chatto and Windus, 1907).

Our book falls into three sections. The first two chapters present a rationale for a multicultural approach to teaching mathematics. The third chapter aims to show, by a collection of brief examples, how such an approach can be applied within and throughout the core of any school curriculum. Finally, the remaining four chapters discuss in greater detail selected topics in elementary arithmetic, algebra, geometry, and statistics.

Our primary aim has been to concentrate on the possibilities for the classroom. We do make suggestions for practical implementation but have refrained from much elaboration for two reasons. First, given the range of teaching methods available and the wide applicability of the material, detailed advice on classroom practice runs the risk of futile prescriptiveness. Secondly, the fragmentary evidence we have accumulated suggests that any well-equipped teacher can use a multicultural approach.

While the volume is the outcome of much discussion, we felt it important that the chapters should be individually written. While sharing a common purpose, we did not want to muffle a healthy diversity of styles of writing and approaches to mathematics and its teaching. We trust the reader will note our consonances, relish our dissonances, and condone the occasional overlap and repetition.

In some quarters the phrase 'multicultural mathematics' induces visions of a rhetorical, educationally unsound vehicle for antiracism. It would be unfortunate if our efforts, tempered by thirty-three years of primary- and secondary-school teaching experience, were prejudged in this way. But, for a work which seeks to show that mathematics has a rich cultural heritage and that it can be taught from a multicultural standpoint, it is difficult to find a more appropriate title.

We are grateful to Dr Alan Bishop, Dr Mary Searle-Chatterjee, Dr Alex Robertson, and also to Malcolm Birkett of Spurley Hey High School for commenting on parts of the manuscript. We are indebted also to the students and teachers who have participated in our courses or helped in other ways, in particular to Richard Bagot, Jane Baker, Martin Bamber, Sharon Cohen, Peter Daly, Kieran Doyle, Alan Jasper, Peter Jones, Robert Munro, Mohammed Nawaz, and Usha Patel. I also gratefully acknowledge help with sources of material from Professor van der Waerden of Zurich and Jean-Luc Verley of Paris.

We are indebted to authors and publishers for the use of copyright material reproduced or adapted with permission in the following: Figures 2.2, 3.1, 3.2, 3.5, 3.6, 3.21, 3.26, 3.27, 3.29, 3.30, 5.5, 6.2(a), 6.2(b), 6.17, 6.23, 6.26, and 7.1. In Figure 6.17, the details from two drawings by M. C. Escher, 'Symmetry Drawing E 105' (1959) and 'Symmetry Drawing E 96' (1955), are included by permission of Collection Haags Gemeentemuseum—The Hague, © M. C. Escher/Cordon Art, Baarn, Holland. Every effort has been made to obtain permission from relevant copyright holders. The publishers would like to hear from copyright holders of any material reproduced in this book which is not properly acknowledged.

Finally, I thank the delegates and staff of Oxford University Press for their patient enthusiasm and skill at all stages in the production of the book.

DAVID NELSON

University of Manchester
October 1991

Contents

1 A Rationale for a Multicultural Approach to Mathematics

GEORGE GHEVERGHESE JOSEPH

Introduction

For many, 'multicultural education' remains a fuzzy concept—a catch-all term covering a variety of issues and practices demanded of, or approved by, the British educational establishment. These include provisions for English or 'mother-tongue' teaching in schools with a strong minority presence, catering for the special dietary needs of certain groups, finding 'space' for non-Christian religions in the classroom and school assembly, the provision of single-sex schools for certain cultural or religious groups, and the elimination of ethnocentrism or racial bias in the curriculum and school texts. It is with the last of these objectives that the issues raised in this book may be seen to have some links.

This lack of clarity in the concept of multicultural education is not merely because it is expected to describe a whole series of unrelated activities. The real problem is that, in the conceptions of both 'education' and 'culture',* there exists a number of definitions and points of disagreement. Depending on the stated objectives of education, we construct a meaning and rationale for different views of multicultural education. Thus, if the emphasis in education is on the development of individual autonomy, a knowledge of different ways of life or world views helps to widen individual choice

---

* It is not our intention here to enter into the controversy regarding the precise meaning of culture. The relationship between a people who possess a culture and the culture itself is highly complex and very germane to the point discussed. The term 'culture' will be used in this chapter in a static and somewhat ambiguous sense to describe a collection of customs, rituals, beliefs, tools, mores, etc., possessed by a group of people who may be related to one another by factors such as a common language, religion, geographical contiguity, or class.

and thereby increase the scope for greater autonomy. If, however, education is seen in instrumental terms as providing skills, including 'language-games', a multicultural approach helps children to negotiate their way around culturally diverse communities.

Alternatively, if the purpose of education is seen primarily in terms of the development of rationality, the question arises as to whose rationality and whether rationality is itself not context-dependent. A child 'inducted' into a variety of cultures would, according to this viewpoint, be able to understand and operate under different forms of rationality. This manner of argument is difficult to sustain, especially since intercultural contact often results in a battle of visions.

There is another approach, which views multicultural education as akin to a 'family-resemblance' concept. We are convinced that we know what it is, but, like the blind persons in the Indian fable touching different parts of an elephant, we fail to recognize the whole elephant. Rather than attempting to identify the purposes of education, we can take a more pragmatic line and find out what an association of the ideas of multiculture and education would produce.

It is possible to distinguish between three distinctive concepts that result from such an association: education *through* many cultures, education *into* many cultures, and education *for* many cultures.

In the first concept—education *through* cultures—the idea is that multicultural elements should permeate all aspects of schooling. The elements that are selected, and why or how they are presented, depend crucially on a teacher's views as to what is attainable and how desirable it is to highlight cultural differences. A teacher who believes that knowledge of and empathy with several cultures is essential for the mental health of children living in a multicultural neighbourhood sees the relevance of multicultural education only for schools in that neighbourhood. The multicultural curriculum is perceived as an essential ingredient in securing emotional security, self-respect, or social harmony in that neighbourhood. If, however, the use of multicultural materials is viewed as a pleasant addition to school life, helpful in entertaining children during the lean periods of the school year, the clear implication is that such materials are neither educationally nor psychologically necessary.

There is another perspective which sees the inclusion of multi-cultural elements as a *moral* necessity. Regardless of whether the use of materials from several cultures is necessary, their inclusion is indicative of a concern about the development of a child's attitude to himself or herself and to others, about creating an environment in which the equal educational treatment and opportunity of minority children is assured, or about promoting better race relations in general.

In the second concept, multicultural education is used to mean education *into* many cultures. Here the idea is that knowledge and understanding of other cultures is worthwhile for its own sake. It is argued that an understanding of one's own culture depends upon a knowledge of other cultures, with which it can be compared and through which we can see what is often taken for granted. However, a distinction should be drawn here between education *about* other cultures and education *into* other cultures. Knowledge about other cultures may bring more understanding and respect. But for empathy to develop there must be a form of *affective* commitment, even involving 'initiation' into other cultures. Whether this is practicable, desirable, or attainable as an educational objective remains a moot point.

The third meaning of multicultural education is education *for* many cultures (i.e. for a multicultural society). This may even be interpreted as a radical concept, in that education is seen as playing an important role in the creation of a just society. The implicit assumptions are that the present society is unjust in certain important aspects. Prejudice is institutionalized. The only option open to minority groups is to integrate—and that is not a genuine synthesis of cultures, but the adoption by minorities of majority culture. This view of multicultural education involves a notion of education which is wider than the ones previously discussed, in that many more practical implications follow. It is not just a case of bringing several cultures into the educational process; it involves all those changes that follow from a realization that education is yet one more important sphere in which racism exists. This realization is often combined with a desire to rectify that state of affairs.

The main practical implication of the first conceptions of multicultural education just discussed is that teachers should acquire substantial knowledge of other cultures if they are to operate effectively in the classroom, including confronting difficult philosophical questions connected with culture clash or incompatibility. But a fundamental question remains: Do 'culturally neutral' criteria exist which allow the choice between alternative forms of reasoning or value systems to enable one to pick the best, no matter where this occurs? But then, if the standards of rationality are themselves culture-bound, a further question arises: Are they equally valid in making curriculum choices? We pose these questions in the typical manner of the academic, without providing the answers!

In the third conception of multicultural education these questions are less important than the wider ones raised by the conflation of 'ethnicity' and 'education' issues. These include the effect on self-image of negative evaluation, the ethnocentric bias in books and materials, and the effect of teacher attitudes and expectations on the performance of minority children. This approach comes closest to what is sometimes described as 'anti-racist education'.

Anti-racist education emerged during the late 1960s when parents, mainly of children of West Indian origin, became increasingly critical of British schools, which, they felt, were failing to educate their children to compete in the wider world on an equal footing with their white peers. There was a sense of disenchantment among many of these immigrants of the first generation, who felt that, however bad things were for them, equality of opportunity in education would counter the effects of racism that was their everyday experience. In 1971 Bernard Coard published his highly influential book entitled *How the West Indian Child is made Educationally Subnormal in the British School System*. Coard argued that the general underachievement of children of West Indian origin lay partly in the way that white teachers responded to their presence in the classroom, with low expectations, lack of understanding, and straight prejudice, and partly in the ethnocentric school curricula (including the 'hidden' curriculum outside the classroom), which had a damaging effect on the children's self-image and motivation.

Coard's influential critique marked the beginnings of a movement which saw not only the mushrooming of organizations of teachers and parents, such as the National Association for Multiracial Education (NAME) and the All London Teachers against Racism and Fascism (ALTARF), but also the setting-up of supplementary schools by concerned parents, mainly in London. There was also growing criticism of the concept of multiculturalism in education. While there are important differences in the critiques offered by different writers (Dhondy 1978; Carby 1980; Mullard 1985), a unifying theme in their works is their perception that a multiculturalist approach is little more than the state response to the struggle against racism in schools. The state response took the form of subtle social control which allowed the promotion of peripheral extra-curricular activities (described vividly as the Sari, Samoosa, and Steelband syndrome), or tinkering with the curriculum by introducing marginalized subjects (such as black studies or comparative religion), while keeping the lid firmly on any radical innovation in classroom curriculum or practice.

Stone's (1981) critique of multicultural education is primarily concerned with the long-term ill-effects of these activities. It starts from the premiss that multiculturalism has serious adverse effects, namely the dangers of providing poor and ill-conceived child-centred education based on dubious considerations, such as enhancing the positive self-images of black children or creating more respect for black cultures. This, the argument continues, is at the expense of teaching them skills required to operate more effectively in life and work situations after school. Stone's arguments amount essentially to a plea for more traditional education, bringing teachers back to teaching the knowledge and skills essential to life in society.

The undoubted value of the anti-racist criticisms has been seriously marred by a simplistic tendency present in all these criticisms: to view multicultural education as a homogeneous and undifferentiated entity, with the state acting as an all-powerful conspiratorial institution bent on controlling the unruly elements in the black population. The truth may lie closer to the motives behind the introduction of multicultural policies, at least at the local government level. And this is the desire to win support from both black parents and white progressive opinion by following policies in which the schools are seen to be fair to all their children. This is the powerful thrust of the Swann Report (1985),*

---

* The Swann Report, entitled *Education for All*, stresses the educational benefits to be derived from highlighting racial and cultural diversity in schools. It sees the primary goal of achieving equality of educational opportunity for all, regardless of sex, race, creed, and class, as perfectly consistent with the promotion of cultural pluralism.

and it is perfectly consistent with a tradition of liberal education found for much of the post-war period in Britain. So the failure of multicultural education, like the failure of comprehensive education to correct for class inequalities, should be viewed in a wider context than the school itself. And that is the manner in which the meritocratic ideal founders on the contradictions endemic within the socio-economic system itself.

In this book, our implicit notion of multicultural education is an amalgam of the three prescriptions examined earlier:

1. Education must (logically) incorporate material from several cultures.
2. Education must incorporate material from several cultures to be effective.
3. Education ought (morally) to incorporate such material not primarily to enhance the self-image of minority children but to help *all* children in the future to negotiate more effectively in a multicultural environment.

The rationale

On the face of it, mathematics does not appear to be a promising subject for multicultural education. There is a view prevalent among mathematics teachers that the universal character of the language and reasoning of mathematics is sufficient evidence of its lack of cultural specificity. After all, whether it is in Shanghai or Timbuktu, the following results are equally valid:

1. Two plus two equals four.
2. A negative quantity multiplied by a negative quantity gives a positive quantity.
3. For all quadrilaterals, the sum of the interior angles adds up to 360 degrees.

There is no arguing with these facts. Mathematical truths, such as these, are universally valid. But then the question arises: Why 'degrees'? or Why is the sum 360 and not 100? The answer: *either* delve into history *or* dismissively respond: 'Some people in the past determined that they should be so. This is not a history lesson.'

In any case the common internal logic and language of mathematics do mask certain cultural differences, in counting, reckoning, and measuring, in the conception of space, and in the logic of grouping and classification. As teachers, we need to recognize the existence of 'alternative' arithmetics and geometries, probably not as well developed as 'mainstream mathematics', which was in any case mainly a cultural product of the last three centuries of European history. We will go part of that way if we recognize that the term 'mathematics' has both a generic use (in the sense that we use terms such as 'language', 'religion', or 'culture') and a specific use, which is rooted in different cultural histories. Such a distinction will help in understanding that all cultures produce mathematical ideas, just as they help to create different languages, religions, and kinship systems. Or, in other words, mathematical pursuits are firmly rooted in a multicultural context. To recognize this fact itself would enhance classroom work.

There are other benefits that accrue from a multicultural approach to mathematical activity in a classroom. At a fairly obvious though superficial level, to recognize and value the cultural heritage of minority pupils helps to build their confidence and pride regarding their background, of which some have ambivalent reactions. But, far more important, by increasing the awareness of *all* children to different cultures, the teacher is helping to overcome the existing deep-rooted Eurocentric bias relating to the origins and practice of mathematics (and science and technology) which subtly affects the attitudes of the vast majority of the population of the United Kingdom regarding populations outside Europe and her cultural dependencies.

The teaching of mathematics should relate both to a child's immediate experience of his or her everyday social and physical environment and to the wider society of which he or she is a part. A good teacher would do this as a matter of course, although the multicultural dimension introduced by the presence of significant minority groups is often ignored in the choice of everyday illustrations. Using the names of members of minority communities in classroom examples, encouraging the publication of texts that deal sensitively with the presence of different ethnic groups in the illustrations, and recognizing the existence of different mensuration systems, calendars, and monetary systems in other countries enhances classroom work. Mathematics is then seen, not as remote textbook abstractions, but as an important human activity.

A multicultural approach helps to promote a 'holistic' view of learning. For example, exploration of the world of Islamic art and design serves to bring together, into a classroom, the mathematical, historical, aesthetic, and religious dimensions of a fascinating world. Islamic designs not only introduce spatial notions of pattern, symmetry, transformation, and equivalence, but also have spin-offs in other school subjects, notably art, religious studies, history, and social studies.

Finally, a multicultural perspective is an invaluable aid to an education in awareness, not only of the physical and social environment in which children operate, but also of their heritage, which contains components other than the European one.

The historical dimension

At a conference of mathematics educators in the United Kingdom, the discussion turned to the perennial topic—the *nature* of mathematics. The arguments were highly abstract and wide-ranging, but what was interesting from a multicultural angle was the *mode* of argument and the framework of discourse. It was not difficult to recognize their highly Eurocentric character, including frequent references to the Greeks and the implicit linking of mathematics and philosophy, which was also a characteristically Greek concern. An implied unquestioned assumption shared by most participants was that philosophical concepts such as knowledge, existence, and truth fell within the scope of any discussion on mathematics. The discussants seemed impervious to other frames of references, such as the close association that existed between the development of mathematics and of linguistics in ancient India, or the role of spatial intuition in the creation of geometric designs in African cultures. Faced by an overwhelmingly Eurocentric frame of reference, one useful device is to switch mentally to a different mode and examine the arguments from other cultural reference points.

The statement by one discussant that 'mathematics does not take place on the street' brought to mind the great eleventh-century

Islamic scientist and philosopher, Ibn Sina (AD 980–1037) (or Avicenna as he came to be known in Europe), who claimed that he had learnt the new (Indian) arithmetic from a street vegetable vendor! Also, anyone familiar with the street scenes of south India three decades ago would have observed astrologers engaged in incredible mental arithmetic, using methods akin to Vedic multiplication (to be discussed in Chapter 4). To the point made by some that mathematics illuminates the meaning of notions such as existence and truth, the cautionary words of the Indian mathematician Mahavira (fl. AD 850) are especially relevant. He argued against engaging in sterile speculations in mathematics which revolved around linguistic definitions. After all, linguistic philosophy made its first appearance in India two thousand years before it won converts in Europe.

The discussion did highlight, if only by omission, certain real differences between Greek (or standard European) and other views on mathematical knowledge. Most mathematical discourses in the Western tradition are carried out with clear reference to some formal deductive system, although the discourse itself might be in the 'informal' mode reminiscent of early Chinese or Indian mathematics. More importantly, the ideal view of Western-inspired mathematics is based on another major philosophical presupposition, that mathematics constitutes a body of infallible or absolute truths. And it is this quest for securing absolute certainty of mathematical knowledge which has motivated many of the foundational investigations into the nature of mathematics and thereby shaped the entire course of mathematics from the Greeks to the present day.

The Indian (or, for that matter, the Chinese) epistemological position on the nature of mathematics is very different. The aim is not to build up an imposing edifice on a few self-evident axioms but to validate a result by any method, including visual demonstration. Thus, some of the notable work in Indian and Chinese mathematics, such as summation of different series or derivation of infinite series, or exposition of the Pythagorean theorem, involve the use of visual demonstrations (or *sredhiksetras* in Sanskrit). These demonstrations are not formulated with any reference to a formal deductive system—and, to a number of historians of mathematics, here lies the fatal flaw in much of non-European mathematics. 'You see they had no proofs, as we know them in modern mathematics. So, were their contributions really mathematics?'

The notion of proof has changed over time and there is by no means a consensus on what constitutes proof. Consider the following problem and the solution offered (expressed in present-day language) of a quadratic in a Babylonian tablet from about 3,500 years ago:

The length of a rectangle exceeds its width by 7 units. Its area is 60 square units. Find its length and width.

In symbolic algebra, the problem is:

$$x(x + 7) = 60 \quad \text{or} \quad x^2 + 7x = 60$$

where x is the width of the rectangle. The solution indicated in the text is:

Halve the quantity by which the length exceeds width (i.e. 3.5). Square 3.5. To the result add area (i.e. 60). Find the square root of this sum. Subtract 3.5 from this square root (i.e. 8.5) to get the width as 5 units. Add 3.5 to the square root to get the length as 12 units.

The modern symbolic form of the solution for the width is:

If $$x^2 + bx = c$$

then $$x = \sqrt{(b/2)^2 + c} - (b/2)$$

Can we claim that the Babylonians were not aware of this general form of the solution, even if they did not express it in symbolic terms? 'A non-symbolic argument or proof can be quite rigorous when given for a particular value of the variable; the conditions for rigour are that the particular value of the variable should be typical, and that a generalisation to any value should be immediate' (Gillings 1972: 233).

It is possible to distinguish between logically deductive and axiomatically deductive algebraic reasoning. The possibility of building up algebra on a set of limited axioms came only after David Hilbert (1862–1943) and Bertrand Russell (1872–1970) had laid down the foundations of mathematical logic. And this was after the emergence of calculus had induced a sea change in attitudes, resulting in a movement away from the mathematics of powerful and ingenious techniques to a mathematics of clear definition and rigorous proofs.

Indeed, we could argue that great mathematicians such as Euler (1707–83), Gauss (1777–1855), and Lagrange (1736–1813) produced 'proofs' which were of the logically deductive variety, closer to the methods of the Chinese and Indians rather than those of their European counterparts two centuries later. An examination of the evidence from non-European sources, including Egyptian and Babylonian mathematics, reveals the presence of considerable technical facility in computations; a recognition of the applicability of certain procedures to a similar set of problems; and an appreciation of the importance of verifying the correctness of a procedure by checking (e.g. a division by multiplication, or the solution of an equation by substitution of the calculated value of the unknown into the original equation). The presence of these procedures and checks in the mathematics of these cultures is indicative of a form of 'proof' in a broad sense. The following remark by a major twentieth-century mathematician is revealing:

There is, strictly, no such thing as mathematical proof; we can, in the last analysis, do nothing but point; proofs are what Littlewood and I call 'gas', rhetorical flourishes designed to affect psychology, pictures on the board in the lecture, devices to stimulate the imagination of pupils. (Hardy 1929: 18)

The Indian view concerning the nature of mathematical objects, such as numbers, appears to be based on a framework developed by Indian logicians (and linguists) and differs significantly at the foundational level from the set-theoretic universe of modern mathematics. None of the major schools of Western thought—Platonism, Formalism, or Intuitionism—gives a satisfactory account of what indeed is the nature of objects (such as numbers) and how they are related to (other) objects in everyday life. It is an arguable point, which I will not develop here, that the Indian view of such objects, if sufficiently researched, may lead to some interesting insights on the nature of mathematical knowledge and its validation. Irrespective of whether this point can be substantiated or not, a more balanced discussion of different epistemological approaches to

Fig. 1.1. The 'classical' Eurocentric trajectory

mathematics would be invaluable. However, a different insight into some of the foundational aspects of the subject is hindered by the prevalence of the Eurocentric view on the historical development of mathematics found in many texts which we will now examine—if only briefly, since a more detailed discussion is found in Joseph (1987, 1991).

The 'classical' Eurocentric trajectory is presented in Fig. 1.1. According to this trajectory, mathematical development is seen as taking place in two areas—Greece, from about 600 BC to AD 300, and post-Renaissance Europe, from the fifteenth century to the present day—separated by a period of stagnation lasting for a thousand years. This intervening period of inactivity was labelled as the 'Dark Ages'—a convenient label which was an expression both of post-Renaissance prejudices about the immediate past and of the intellectual self-confidence of those who saw themselves as the true inheritors of the 'Greek miracle' that had occurred on the Ionian soil two thousand years earlier. This view of history served as a useful rationale for a colonial ideology of dominance in the past. Traces of it still remain today, despite ample evidence of significant mathematical developments in Mesopotamia, Egypt, China, pre-Columbian America, India, and the Arab world, and despite further evidence that Greek mathematics owed a significant debt to the mathematics of some of those cultures.

A somewhat grudging acceptance of the debt owed by Greek mathematicians to earlier civilizations, and of the seminal contributions of the Arabs, has led some historians of mathematics in recent years to accept the 'modified' Eurocentric trajectory shown in Fig. 1.2. However, this figure takes no account of the contributions of India, China, and other cultures. Even in those texts where the mathematics of the first two areas are discussed, the discussion is often confined to a single chapter, which may go under the misleading title of 'oriental' mathematics. There is little in-

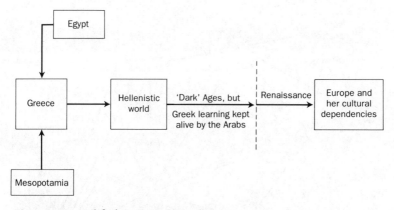

Fig. 1.2. A modified Eurocentric trajectory

dication of how these cultures contributed to the mainstream development of mathematics and no attempt to take account of recent research into the mathematics of these and other areas. They are included in histories of mathematics as a 'residual dump', to be ignored without affecting the main story.

There is also no indication in Fig. 1.2 of the routes through which Hellenistic, Chinese, Indian, and Arab mathematical works arrived in Europe. Fig. 1.3 provides an 'alternative' trajectory of such transmissions between the eighth and fifteenth centuries, the period described as the 'Dark Ages'. The cross-transmission between different cultural areas, and the critical role of the Arabs in taking mathematics westwards, are illustrated in the diagram. They will not be discussed here, the interested reader may wish to consult Joseph (1991).

There are certain lessons to be learnt for the classroom from a less Eurocentric perspective to mathematical development. We will consider just two.

First, it is important to point out the misleading aspects of naming mathematical results only after Greeks and Europeans. For example, the earliest known demonstrations of the theorem of Pythagoras are found in an ancient Chinese text, *Chou Pei*, conservatively dated around the latter half of the first millennium BC and in the *Sulbasutras* (c.800–500 BC) from India. Antecedents

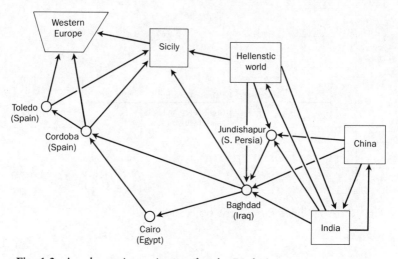

Fig. 1.3. An alternative trajectory for the Dark Ages

of Pascal's triangle, Gregory's series, or the Ruffini–Horner method are all found outside Europe.

Secondly, if we accept the principle (stated on p. 7) that teaching should be tailored to students' experience of the social and physical environment in which they live, mathematics should draw on these experiences, including the mathematical heritage of different ethnic minority groups in Britain. The *rangoli* patterns which decorate the homes of Hindu and Sikh families, the geometric art which forms the basis of the Islamic designs in mosques and wall coverings, the calendars which determine the Jewish and Chinese new year are all part of the rich heritage which can be brought to life in a mathematics lesson. Drawing on the traditions of these groups, indicating that their cultures are recognized and valued, would also help to counter the entrenched historical devaluation of them. Again, by promoting such an approach, mathematics is brought into contact with a wide range of disciplines, including art and design, history and social studies, which it conventionally ignores. Such a holistic approach would serve to augment rather than fragment a child's understanding and imagination.

Social and political values shaping a mathematics curriculum

Consider the range of topics on offer in a school mathematics curriculum. There are good social reasons for including topics such as social arithmetic, numeracy skills, measures, ratio and proportion, variation, and percentages. However, there is no strong *mathematical* justification for studying, say, percentages. Percentages are taught in the classroom for social and practical reasons, including servicing the commercial and financial sectors. Similarly, the current enthusiasm for computers and other technological tools has no overwhelmingly mathematical rationale. It is the valuing of new technology and the perception that knowledge of such usage would enhance work skills that underline much of the enthusiasm for these technological aids.

There can be no doubt that questions on stocks and shares, which were common in school mathematics during the 1950s and 1960s, gave legitimacy to an activity of which the overwhelming number of children had little experience. Similarly, questions about bath filling and emptying of earlier decades must have appeared remote to many children who did not have such a facility at home. Indeed, the highly influential Cockcroft Report (1982: Para. 462) stated that 'Mathematics lessons in secondary schools are very often not about anything.'

The current controversy among educators about the uses of school mathematics, stimulated by the adoption of the National Curriculum, is strangely reminiscent of the debate in England about one hundred years ago on the purposes of education for the masses. There existed then three different views on the curriculum for the masses. The first group, the 'employer' lobby, was emphatic that education should serve the perceived needs of industry and commerce within the economy. The 'public-education' lobby was concerned with the growth and development of the whole individual, and education for democratic citizenship. The academic (or 'humanist') lobby argued that subjects should be studied for their own sake, that the transmission of knowledge and the communication of a specific academic discipline to a student was a justification in itself.

When science was first introduced into English education around the middle of the nineteenth century, there was a move led by certain educationalists, notably Dawes and Moseley, to devise a curriculum which called upon the experience and knowledge of a student's everyday life. This approach, described by Layton (1973) as the 'science of common things', involved teaching science through common-day problems of cottage ventilation, personal hygiene, family nutrition, and gardening. This was an approach consistent with that of the 'public-education' perspective, though some concessions were made to the other lobbies by emphasizing, for the benefit of the 'humanist' lobby, the objective of raising students 'into the scale of thinking beings' (Layton 1973: 189) and, for the 'employer' lobby, the vocational usefulness of scientific knowledge. The lobby promoting the 'science of common things' lost.

The reasons given by those who opposed this approach to the science curriculum are interesting. First, and this was clearly implied if not stated, the idea of giving the masses access to practical scientific knowledge, which some of the members of the upper classes did not possess, was seen as subverting the existing social order. Secondly, liberal educators argued that a curriculum selected because of its immediate utility to a particular social group (in this instance the working classes) might lead to a 'ghetto curriculum' in which pupils would be discouraged from looking beyond their own environment. Thirdly, modern sciences and their industrial applications were thought to be best served by the application of mathematics to scientific problems, especially in the case of physics. The mathematization of science was seen as the very antithesis of the 'science of common things'.

The parallels between the nineteenth-century debate on the science curriculum and the present-day deliberations on mathematics education are there to be seen. If a mathematics educator is asked the reasons for including mathematics as a core subject in the curriculum, the arguments rehearsed will follow along familiar lines. Mathematics is perceived as offering a rigorous training in rational thought by extending logical and critical thinking and problem-solving abilities. This argument, in spite of justifiable scepticism on the part of many who are directly involved in teaching and learning mathematics, is essentially the old 'humanist' position. The analogy with the 'employer' lobby is in the argument that the primary purpose of mathematics education is to deliver skilled manpower (and more recently womanpower) to the workplace; and there are frequent complaints on the part of employers and politicans about failure on this front. The final argument is the significant contribution of mathematics to the growth, development, and general education of a whole individual, a citizen who is expected to make informed judgements on various aspects of society on the basis, among other things, of statistics and quantitative indicators. This is an approach wholly consistent with the idea of science education promoted by Dawes, Moseley, and the 'public-education' lobby in the middle of the last century and may be described as the 'mathematics of common things'.

An important question that arises in examining the three perspectives is what each one of them implies about the relationship between mathematics and society. The academic (or 'humanist') approach does not acknowledge any substantive 'social' dimension in the study of mathematics. The utilitarian (or 'employer') approach recognizes a one-way relationship between mathematics and the outside world—mathematics is an input into training for specific skills and expertise. Both these approaches have had a significant influence on the mathematics curriculum of this country. As a consequence, there is a tendency to see mathematics as 'free' of social considerations and values. This perception, as we shall argue later, is a major obstacle to the introduction of a balanced mathematics curriculum.

The third perspective allows for a more dynamic and interactive relationship between mathematics and society. It is built on a view of society which takes account of different constituencies of interest, including the specific cultural interest of the learner. The real danger with this approach is that, if one defines an excessively narrow constituency of interests for which a mathematics curriculum is then constructed, there could result a 'ghetto curriculum', devaluing both the content and the context of the mathematics learnt. This is the danger uppermost in the minds of parents, teachers, and employers when faced with curriculum reform, including attempts to provide a multicultural dimension to mathematics education. One way of safeguarding against this danger is to emphasize both the practical uses of mathematics and its relevance as a developing universal language and discipline. It is here that a historical approach could pay dividends. And this is precisely what the multicultural examplars discussed later in this book hope to provide.

Objectives

In 1987, at the Annual Conservative Party Conference, Prime Minister Margaret Thatcher declared: 'Children who need to count and multiply are being taught anti-racist mathematics, whatever that may be.' Mrs Thatcher's puzzlement is shared by many, including a number of teachers. Multicultural/Anti-racist (MC/AR) mathematics is perceived as a strange and incongruous subject introduced into an already over-laden mathematics syllabus, rather than as an approach which permeates all topics within the syllabus.

This view is best captured in the section on ethnic and cultural diversity (paragraphs 10.18–10.23) of the National Curriculum Report (DES 1988) entitled *Mathematics for Ages 5 to 16.*

It is sometimes suggested that the multi-cultural complexion of society demands a 'multi-cultural' approach to mathematics with children being introduced to different numeral systems, foreign currencies and non-European measuring and counting devices. We are concerned that undue emphasis on multi-cultural mathematics, in these terms, could confuse young children. While it is right to make clear to children that mathematics is the product of a diversity of cultures, priority must be given to ensuring that they have the knowledge, understanding and skills which they will need for adult life and employment in Britain in the twenty-first century. We believe that most ethnic parents will share this view. (para. 10.20)

Many of those who argue for a multi-cultural approach to the mathematics curriculum do so on the basis that such an approach is necessary to raise the self-esteem of ethnic minority cultures and to improved mutual understanding and respect between races. We believe that this attitude is misconceived and patronising. (para. 10.22)

These quotations summarize well the widespread reservations that exist about multicultural mathematics. It is seen as something irrelevant or peripheral, a sop for, even patronizing, ethnic minority children, not particularly useful in providing training for adult life and employment, educationally unsound because it may confuse children. It involves adding extra bits to the existing curriculum which would further burden teachers and children. At a special conference convened to respond to the sections on ethnic and cultural diversity in the National Curriculum documents on mathematics and science, we recommended that Paragraph 10.20 quoted above, should be replaced by:

The mathematics curriculum must provide opportunities for all pupils to recognize that all cultures engage in mathematical activity and no single culture has a monopoly on mathematical achievement. All pupils must be given the opportunity to enrich their mathematical experience by selection of appropriate materials to stimulate and develop the knowledge, understanding, and skills which they will need for adult life and employment in Britain in the twenty-first century. Mathematical experience may be enriched by examples from a variety of cultures—e.g. Vedic arithmetic enhances understanding of number, Islamic art patterns are based on complex geometric construction, and the Chinese had a rod numeral method of solving simultaneous equations that leads naturally to methods used in higher mathematics.

We quote this passage in full for two reasons. First, it introduces the exemplars of multicultural mathematics which will be discussed later in the book. Secondly, it also conveys by implication what we identify as the 'hidden' objective of promoting the permeation of multiculturalism into the mathematics curriculum. The multicultural approach to mathematics is best seen as part of a general strategy of making mathematics more accessible and less anxiety-arousing among a wider public. It challenges the overall content and pedagogy of the standard curriculum in its signal failure to make mathematics more accessible to working class, female, and black students. It counters the view that mathematics consists of a sequence of unconnected skills, taught in isolation from the real world of applications, and prepares those who have the ability and commitment to join a tiny inward group, speaking the language of, and sharing their enthusiasm for, the subject. The vast majority, however, after their experience at school, become defensive about their poor performance in the subject and their relief to be rid of it once they leave school.

It is possible to distinguish four overlapping objectives in pursuing a multicultural approach to mathematics (Mathematical Association 1989: 4–9).

1. Drawing on a Child's Own Experience as a Resource

Certain abstract concepts of mathematics can be given a concrete form by well-chosen examples which are familiar to the class. The overriding consideration in the choice of objects or examples should always be mathematical. In a class containing children from Hindu or Sikh households, the *rangoli* patterns used to decorate their houses on festive days serve as a useful introduction to geometrical notions of pattern, symmetry, transformations, and equivalence. For children belonging to Islamic and Jewish faiths, time measurement involving the principles of constructing calendars and demarcation of eras, including the role of lunar calendars, could be developed from a few questions regarding the religious practices of these groups. An ability to convert from one system of recording time to another would not only be a useful exercise in arithmetic, but would help all children to appreciate the diversity of their local environment. For example, they could now understand why their Chinese and Jewish neighbours do not have their New Year's Day on 1 January. Time measurement is discussed further in Chapter 3.

2. Recognizing Different Cultural Heritages

There is a practical limit to how much of a child's own experience can be drawn on in learning mathematics. But cultural heritage is a different matter and, if used imaginatively, is an exciting way of learning mathematics. Children are given opportunities to see the development of mathematics as a pan-cultural endeavour. Modern mathematics evolved to its present form as a result of centuries of cross-fertilization of ideas from different cultures. The story of the spread of what is now the universal system of numeration is a fascinating one. Our number system grew out of the work on the Indian subcontinent about two thousand years ago, transmitted south as far as Indonesia, east as far as Cambodia, north as far as Mongolia, and west as far as the British Isles during the next twelve centuries. Manipulations and representations of algebraic quantities, the distinction between rational and irrational numbers, and the evolution of concepts of zero and infinity excited the imaginations of Greek, Indian, Mayan, and Chinese mathematicians.

We owe the foundations of algebra (an Arabic word), the development of trigonometry (the word 'sine' can be traced to the Sanskrit term *jya*), the discovery of the Pascal triangle (known in China five hundred years before Pascal), and the numerical and geometric solutions of higher order equations to civilizations outside Europe. It is this 'international' dimension that should be stressed wherever appropriate in the teaching of school mathematics. It is not suggested that detailed historical investigations should form part of the process of learning mathematics, except where possibilities exist for projects or investigations directed at specific subjects—for example, 'The History of Pi' or 'Egyptian Operations with Unit Fractions' or 'Calculus before Newton'. But there could still be a historical or cultural perspective on mathematics education.

First, all mathematics teachers should have at their fingertips a fund of interesting stories on the origins and development of various topics in mathematics. They could serve as useful diversions, emphasizing the practical origins of mathematics as well as reinforcing the view that mathematics is a universal activity, though often taking culturally specific forms. The collection of such stories and information should be undertaken at the departmental level and incorporated into regular schemes of work. The source of such materials should not be just the standard histories of mathematics, which tend on the whole to be Eurocentric (and Grecocentric), but should include the growing literature on non-European traditions which are mentioned in the Bibliography.

Secondly, there are certain exemplars which provide fresh insights into certain topics. They often contain a new approach or method of solving a specific problem which can be incorporated directly into classroom teaching. An interesting example is the attempt to teach topics by examining historic texts in which they appeared (M:ATH 1986, 1990). Most of the exemplars are taken from standard Greek or European sources. There is a need to widen the sources to include mathematics and mathematicians from other cultural traditions.

3. Combating Racism

The Swann Report (DES 1985) is one of a number of recent reports that has highlighted the existence of racism in both British society and British schools. The mathematics teacher, like teachers of other subjects, needs to be aware of the ways in which racism enters the classroom and how it can be countered. ILEA (1985) gives the following examples of ways in which bias or insensitivity to minorities may creep, however unconsciously, into a mathematics lesson.

Classroom examples unduly restrictive
- Using the common statistics example of ownership of pets in a class with a large number of children of Asian or African origin, among whom keeping pets may be uncommon. The point here is not that such an example should not be used, but that the teacher should be aware of its cultural dimension.

Certain ethnic groups ignored or devalued
- Accepting the stereotype of a West Indian child being 'no good' at mathematics compared to an Asian child.
- Commenting that, before Europeans came, the Africans had a primitive counting system, as that was all that was needed in a simple society.

Insensitivity to the position of minority groups in society
- Refusing to recognize that issues of racial discrimination and power relations within the wider society are proper subjects of study in a mathematics classroom.

4. Promoting 'Socially Desirable' Attitudes

The use of mathematics to affect social attitudes can be illustrated by specific examples from colonial and post-colonial Mozambique. Gerdes (1985: 457, 459) describes how, during Portuguese rule, questions beginning:

> In a factory, men earned 45$, women 30$, and apprentices 15$ . . .

> In Lourenco Marques, Mr Abilo has a house rented to four tenants who pay . . .

contained 'hidden' messages regarding sexual inequality and landlord/tenant relations respectively; similarly, questions beginning:

23 peasants are working in a field. At midday 6 Frelimo guerilla fighters arrive to help them . . .

Yesterday there were 22 women in a literacy class. Today 5 more women joined the class . . .

emphasized the social role of the Frelimo fighters and the importance of literacy for women respectively. The very fact that many teachers would be prepared to accept the first two questions from the colonial period, while having reservations about the political nature of the example that refers to guerila fighters, indicates how problematic is the concept of a value-free mathematics for the classroom.

Mmari (1978: 322) gives the following problems from school textbooks in Tanzania during British colonial rule.

If a cricketer scores altogether r runs in x innings, n times not out, his average is $r/(x - n)$. Find his average if he scores 204 runs in 15 innings, 3 times not out.

The escalator at the Holborn tube station is 156 feet long and makes the ascent in 65 seconds. Find the speed in miles per hour.

Reduce 207,042 farthings, 89,761 half-pence, 6,708 half-shillings to £.s.d.

What children who had never played cricket nor seen an escalator and used a different currency would have made of these examples has not been recorded.

Conclusion

When adopting a multicultural approach to teaching mathematics, two general questions should be asked initially:

- What are the mathematical objectives for introducing a certain topic?
- What is the best approach for achieving these objectives from the points of view of both teaching and learning?

Only after these two questions are resolved should the following questions be asked:

- Is there any multicultural potential to be drawn from the topic? If so, what are the resources required and where are they to be found?

We hope to address these questions in the chapters that follow.

2 Teaching Mathematics from a Multicultural Standpoint

DAVID NELSON

Consider for a moment a class of schoolchildren and their mathematics teacher. The curriculum which is presented and developed in the classroom is the outcome of a number of influences. Some of these may be thought of as *internal*, arising primarily from the pupils or teacher, and others as essentially *external*.

A prime internal influence is the teacher's knowledge and overall view of the subject. Present-day mathematics can be said to be conducted in an international symbolic language which includes a decimal notation for numbers. Both the diagram in Fig. 2.1

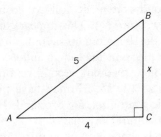

Fig. 2.1.

and the statements $\angle ACB = 90$

and $x^2 + 4^2 = 5^2$

can be taken as universally understood by mathematicians. But we have only arrived at this situation in the last few centuries. Mathematics has a long and intricate history. The first mathemat-

Fig. 2.2. The notched bone of Border Cave, southern Africa (Bogoshi, Naidoo, and Webb 1987)

ical artefacts—the notched bones—come from places as far apart as the Border Cave in southern Africa (35,000 BC) and central Czechoslovakia (30,000 BC) (see Fig. 2.2). The modern fusion was preceded by developments in and transmissions between cultures in Central America, Egypt, Babylon, India, China, Korea, Japan, Greece, and Western Europe. The above mathematical statements exemplify this diversity. The use of 360 degrees for a complete revolution goes back to the Babylonian sexagesimal (60-based) number system, the notation for the angle to the Greeks, the sign for equality to Robert Recorde (1557), the 'plus' sign for addition to Vander Hoecke (1519), the x^2 notation to Descartes (1637), and both the decimal notation and the zero to the Indians and Chinese. The second statement follows from the 'theorem of Pythagoras' (sixth century BC). This appears to have been known and explored by the Babylonians a millenium beforehand and one finds it in such places as the Indian *Sulbasutras* (*c*.800–500 BC) and China (the Gougu theorem, second century BC), and Pythagorean triples such as 12, 35, 37 may have played a part in the design of megalithic stone circles in Scotland. The teacher's subject thus has rich multicultural origins.

Teacher and pupils share life in a multicultural society. Some of them may belong to some of the ethnic minority groups and this diversity of culture is a possible internal source for developing the curriculum. Irrespective of the ethnic mix of the classroom, an external force on the teacher will be the school's general policy on multicultural education, which commonly aims to promote cultural awareness and tolerance amongst pupils and prepare them for life in a multicultural society.

Another internal factor is the shared life of the classroom—the day-to-day 'conversation' of the children and teacher. They work and play together, sharing successes and disappointments. A resourceful teacher can sometimes link this to the curriculum. Personal experiences, within the school or locality, national or international events, questions the children ask—all these may present opportunities for numerate discussion at the least and in some cases conceptual development. The belief 'If footballer Ian Rush scores a goal in a match, then Liverpool (his club) are almost certain not to lose' provides a vivid introduction to the idea of conditional probability. In this case it can involve a comparison of the probability that Liverpool lose a match, the probability that they lose a match in which they have scored, and the probability that they lose a match in which Rush scores. The day-to-day 'conversation' may involve both mathematical and cultural issues, e.g. 'Where does the word *algebra* come from?',* 'How is the date of the start of Ramadan calculated?'†

An important factor in shaping the curriculum is the teacher's command of a range of teaching styles and associated teaching materials. We expect our teacher's methods to include (1) direct instruction and exposition, (2) guided discovery and discussion, and (3) pupil-led investigations. Put another way, we expect the *locus of control* (1) to rest with the teacher, (2) to be shared, and (3) to rest with the pupils. To this list we should add cross-curricular initiatives and also projects which involve parents or other members of the local community. The materials in this book are best exploited by using a variety of teaching styles.

* The title of Al-Khwarizmi's book *Hisab al-jabr w'al-muqabala* (Calculation by Restoration and Reduction), later abbreviated and transliterated to *Algebra*, highlights two key processes used in solving equations: *jabr* eliminates a negative quantity from one side by adding (or restoring) a positive amount to the other side, thus turning

$$14 - 2x = 4 + 3x$$

into $$14 = 4 + 3x + 2x = 4 + 5x$$

muqabala reduces each side of an equation by the same amount, thus turning

$$14 = 4 + 5x$$

into $$10 = 5x$$

The name, Al-Khwarizmi, of this Arab mathematician (*c.* AD 780–*c.*850) is the source of the modern term *algorithm*.

† Calendars are discussed in Chapter 1 (p. 20) and Chapter 3 (pp. 67–8).

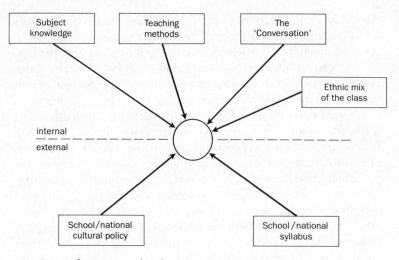

Fig. 2.3. Influences on the classroom

Finally there will be the framework of mathematical aims and objectives, the declared school syllabus, to which the teacher is bound to work and within which the curriculum for pupils is shaped.

The purpose of this simplified discussion of influences on a curriculum is to ask how such a teacher is to operate in a multicultural world. More precisely, should such a teacher give the curriculum a multicultural dimension? This question is the starting-point for the remainder of the chapter. It may help to raise two rather more precise, and also contrasting questions which will guide our discussion:

1. Can cultural materials be found which will enhance a mathematical education?
2. Can mathematical topics be used to contribute towards a multicultural education?

The cultural void

The content of the mathematics curriculum has changed radically in most countries this century. The tools of arithmetic have changed from slide rules and logarithms to sophisticated calculators and computers. The secondary curriculum has altered from a mixture of arithmetic, algebra, geometry, trigonometry, and calculus to one which also introduces ideas of probability and statistics, co-ordinate and vector geometry, investigational work, and applications of mathematics to post-war developments such as linear programming and critical path analysis. In the debates and discussions associated with this transformation, advocacy of a multi-cultural element has been almost entirely absent. By design or otherwise, curriculum discussion has been devoid of cultural considerations and it is only in recent years that Education Ministries have begun to include the word 'culture' in their general aims. Thus one has the French circular of 1986: 'It is advisable to stress the cultural contents of mathematics', and the Danish upper secondary curriculum in 1988: 'The pupils must achieve knowledge of elements of the history of mathematics, and mathematics in cultural and social contexts.'*

There is a curious contrast between the books and papers of professional mathematicians and the reports and syllabuses of the administrators of maths education. The former often contain references to the historical development of the subject in question, achievements of individuals, false trails, and unsolved problems. The latter rarely mention history, individual mathematicians, or cultures. Consequently mathematics does not emerge as a human creation and discovery, and valuable opportunities to promote the role model of mathematician or scientist are missed. In the seventy-five pages it takes to state the National Curriculum† and give illustrative examples and statutory guidance on schemes of work, *Mathematics in the National Curriculum* (DES 1989) contains only two words which indicate human intervention in the development of mathematics—Cartesian and Pythagoras.

The neglect of history

If multiculturalism has been absent, there has been some exhortation over the last hundred years to use history in mathematics

---

* CDE (1986) *Bulletin Officiel*, No. 31 (Paris), 2344; Direktoratet for Gymnasie-skolerne og HF (1988), *Matematik* (Copenhagen), 351.
† The title may mislead some readers; it applies only to England and Wales.

teaching. But apart from notable exceptions, such as the school textbooks of the American W. W. Rupert (1900–1), earlier texts by R. Potts of Trinity College, Cambridge, such as *Elementary Arithmetic, with Brief Notices of its History* (1876), and W. Popp's *History of Mathematics: Topics for Schools* (1978), resolutions and exhortations to use history to improve the teaching of the subject, or enliven the subject-matter, or broaden the knowledge of teachers during training, have had next to no effect on the texts our children study, the examinations they sit,* or the teaching they receive. At the end of a detailed survey of the previous hundred years, David Green (1976*b*: 7) wrote:

Clearly there has been almost no British project or series of texts which has taken seriously the incorporation of historical material into its mathematics and it must be concluded that virtually no pupils at school have met the history of mathematics through their school texts. The level of history in mathematics teacher training suggests that pupils are unlikely to meet it in the classroom.

This contrasts starkly with the Ministry of Education pamphlet *Teaching Mathematics in Secondary Schools* (1958: 134, 154), which declared:

The teacher who knows little of the history of mathematics is apt to teach techniques in isolation, unrelated either to the problems and ideas which generated them or to the further developments which grew out of them . . . Mathematics can be properly taught only against a background of its own history.

The neglect of history is self-perpetuating. One obstacle to its cure is the nature of intellectual history. 'For a theoretical subject *x*, telling the story of *x* is not a conceptually distinct undertaking from describing the theory of *x* . . . The readership of a serious history of *x* will thus be largely limited to the few specialists in *x*, a small circulation at best' (Rota 1986: 157).

Even the excellent general histories by Boyer and Eves can seem daunting to teachers meeting historical material for the first time and to those whose first degree or main qualification was not in

---

* For a time in the 1950s and 1960s history of mathematics appeared as an option in the Ordinary and Advanced syllabuses of a few examination boards, such as the Northern Joint Matriculation Board and the Cambridge Syndicate.

mathematics. These texts call for general knowledge of geography, languages, and history, as well as a sound grasp of mathematics. The enthusiasts for history have perhaps underestimated teachers' difficulties here. A further problem is that much of the mathematics studied at secondary level was discovered in the period up to Newton and Leibniz and there has been an enormous development since then.

A way forward

One of the attractions of a multicultural approach for a teacher with an interest in history is that the non-European cultures flourished in just that period, from the beginning to Newton (1642–1727), when 'school' mathematics was being discovered.

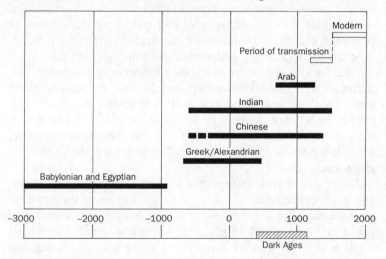

Fig. 2.4. Time map showing main periods of mathematical development in various cultures

The time map (Fig. 2.4) shows Chinese mathematics flourishing up to the thirteenth century; Indian up to the Kerala mathematicians of the sixteenth. The existence of this rich field of African, Middle Eastern, Indian, and Chinese mathematics, whose content is mostly within the compass of school mathematics, to set alongside Greek and early European developments, has considerable potential for school teaching. A favourable development here is that knowledge of non-European mathematics is increasing and becoming more widespread. The example set by the histories of Cajori (1893) and Smith (1923–5) is at last being followed, and general histories are now devoting more space to non-European mathematics. Amongst recent publications, George Gheverghese Joseph's *The Crest of the Peacock* (1991), which is devoted entirely to non-European mathematics, is particularly helpful.

This increase in knowledge places obligations on us. Mathematics requires exact calculation, exact drawing, and exact argument. The teacher who wishes to be exact in attributing discoveries cannot ignore the multicultural dimension. Thus Pascal's triangle of 1645 was in use much earlier in China—in the eleventh century at the latest. A teacher will need to look outside Europe for the first instances of many secondary-school topics: zero, negative numbers, formulae for the areas of triangles and quadrilaterals, volumes of pyramids and frusta, solution of simultaneous equations, quadratic equations, and iterative methods of solution. I am disinclined to take the view that there has been a Eurocentric conspiracy, but harmful and profound misconceptions do exist. Accurate teaching from a multicultural standpoint will meet Joseph Needham's call (1973: 1): 'One of the greatest needs of the world in our time is the growth and wide dissemination of a true historical perspective, for without it whole peoples can make the gravest misjudgements about each other.'

The matter of veracity is part of a wider issue. The multicultural approach enables one to develop the child's grasp of the extent of mathematics. The question 'What did the Babylonians know?' will probably be answered by grouping knowledge and achievements in such areas as number system and arithmetic, measuring and geometry, and algebra. This in turn must encourage a similar organization and overview of the child's own knowledge. Regular structured reviews are important—they strengthen long-term memory and encourage a global view of the subject.

Again, a multicultural approach can lead to a better appreciation of the history of ideas and the evolution of the subject. It comes as a surprise and comfort to many children that negative numbers were at first regarded with fear and suspicion or simply not accepted. Even more important is the development of algebraic notation. At first algebraic arguments were conducted verbally, giving rise to the term *rhetorical* algebra (or *prose* algebra). A typical statement would be 'The square of the unknown quantity is the sum of 6 and 10.' Here are two examples from Al-Khwarizmi's *Algebra*.

If the instance be, 'ten and thing to be multiplied by thing less ten,' then this is the same as if it were said thing and ten by thing less ten. You say, therefore, thing multiplied by thing is a square positive; and ten by thing is ten things positive; and minus ten by thing is ten things negative. You now remove the positive by the negative, then there only remains a square. Minus ten multiplied by ten is a hundred, to be subtracted from the square. This, therefore, altogether, is a square less a hundred dirhems. (1977 edn.: 26)

The elucidation by words is very easy. You know that you have a hundred and a square, minus twenty roots. When you add to this fifty and ten roots, it becomes a hundred and fifty and a square, minus ten roots. The reason for these ten negative roots is, that from the twenty negative roots ten positive roots were subtracted by reduction. This being done, there remains a hundred and fifty and a square, minus ten roots. With the hundred a square is connected. If you subtract from this hundred and square the two squares negative connected with fifty, then one square disappears by reason of the other, and the remainder is a hundred and fifty, minus a square, and minus ten roots.

This it was that we wished to explain. (1977 edn.: 34)

The first example shows

$$(10 + x)(x - 10) = x^2 - 100$$

and the second explains that

$$(100 + x^2 - 20x) + (50 + 10x - 2x^2) = 150 - x^2 - 10x$$

The remarkable achievements of Babylon, Arabia, Greece, Egypt, and India were reached by these means. In the case of the Greeks, the prose was of a geometrical nature. For example, the modern product xyz would have been rendered 'the solid whose sides are the first, second, and third unknown quantity' where 'solid' means 'volume of the cuboid' (see Fig. 2.5). With apparatus such as this, these cultures solved quadratic and some cubic equations.

The next stage was to replace some of the key terms and phrases

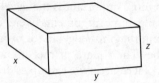

Fig. 2.5. A cuboid with sides x, y, and z

Symbol or expresssion	Modern interpretation
ς	x
Δ^Y	x^2
K^Y	x^3
⋏	minus
$\overset{\circ}{M}$	constant term
$K^Y{}_\alpha\Delta^Y\delta\varsigma\beta$	x^3+4x^2+2x
$\Delta^Y\varepsilon⋏\varsigma\gamma\overset{\circ}{M}\iota$	$5x^2-(3x+10)$

Fig. 2.6. Some elements of Diophantine syncopated algebra

by standard shorthand or abbreviations. The resultant mixture was called *syncopated* algebra.

The pioneer was Diophantus of Alexandria (*c.* AD 250). He developed an algebra, with one unknown, capable of dealing with powers up to the sixth and their reciprocals. Fig. 2.6 gives some examples of this algebra, which used the Greek ciphered system for its numerals (see Heath 1921, vol. ii).

The Indians Aryabhata (*c.* AD 475–*c.*550) and Brahmagupta (*c.* AD 598–*c.*665) took a similar step. Their algebra used *yā* (short for *yāvat tāvat*) for the main unknown, and additional unknowns were given abbreviations of names of colours: e.g. *kā* for *kālaka* (black) and *ni* for *nilaka* (blue). Fig. 2.7 gives some examples in this system.

Rhetorical and syncopated algebra did not begin to be replaced by the fully symbolic algebra we use in schools until the seventeenth century. The development of algebra in the school curriculum

Symbol or expression	Modern interpretation
bha	product
yā	x
kā	y
ka	$\sqrt{}$
•	minus
rū	integer
yā kā 6 bha	$6xy$
ka 5 rū 2̇	$\sqrt{5}-2$

Fig. 2.7. Some elements of Brahmagupta's syncopated algebra

follows the same pattern—from rhetorical to symbolic—but we expect our children to achieve the evolution in ten years and not almost three thousand!* Many children find the transition to symbolic algebra difficult and their difficulties have been the subject of much research. One wonders whether a greater awareness of the evolution of algebra on the part of educators (and the children themselves) would ease matters.

One of the external pressures on the teacher, mentioned at the beginning of this chapter, is the need to implement the school's policy on multicultural education. It will now be seen that the mathematics teacher has ample material with which to make a *non-controversial* contribution. By placing mathematics in its true historical perspective, it is seen as a global enterprise involving many cultures for over four thousand years. Mathematics can also be brought to bear on contemporary society. The collection, display, and analysis of data is a standard curriculum element, and the simple act of obtaining data on, say, the ethnic mix of one's country or town, or the faiths of the world, will contribute to multicultural education.

An important general aim is to improve the child's *affective*

---

* Note also, when beginning calculus, the transition from the rhetorical 'gradient of the curve at a general point' through the syncopated 'grad(x)' to the symbolic $\frac{\text{'}dy\text{'}}{dx}$.

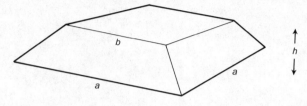

Fig. 2.8. A square plinth

attitude towards mathematics. The multicultural approach can help here, for it provides many episodes of human interest involving individuals or groups. One can relive the failures, dead-ends, discoveries, and debates of mathematics, and promote investigation. For example, here is a challenge: 'The Babylonians used the inexact formula $\frac{1}{2}(a^2 + b^2)h$ for the volume of this square plinth. In the Moscow Papyrus of 1850 BC the Egyptians are using the correct formula. What is it?' (see Fig. 2.8). If you find this problem difficult, a beautiful discussion of a route to its solution is given in Pólya (1965, vol. ii).

Similarly, take the Egyptian and Babylonian rule for the area of a four-sided figure: 'Multiply the averages of the opposite sides.' Under this rule, a trapezium with consecutive sides 6, 10, 6, 8 is given an area of 6×9 or 54, which is incorrect. When *is* the rule correct?

This leads to my final proposal in favour of selective but persistent permeation of teaching with the multicultural element: briefly, it assists teaching. The second part of the book presents some case studies in support of this proposal. Here we generalize.

One direction in which the approach seems promising is that of strengthening concepts. Suppose, from experience of four-sided figures, you have classified some as sharing a property and given them the class name 'trapezium'. You look for further instances of this figure, set it alongside other types of four-sided figures you known—rectangle, parallelogram. You seek out its properties and maybe wonder whether you could have something like a 'trapezium' in three dimensions. In this activity I believe the multicultural approach has little to offer. But consider the important concept of our decimal numeral system. Efforts to enrich and strengthen this concept by setting it alongside other systems are surely assisted by presenting a judicious selection from the enormous variety of systems used in other cultures. A second and more pressing teaching problem is that of the abstract nature of mathematics. To those who can play its game it is intoxicating and the favoured few never look back. But for many the rules lack meaning and the concepts are unclear. In the words of René Thom (1973: 202): 'The real problem which confronts mathematics teaching is not that of rigour, but the problem of the development of "meaning", of the "existence" of mathematical objects.'

This is not the place to debate theories of child development but, whether one is following Piaget, who envisages the child moving from the stage of concrete operations to that of formal operations, or Bruner, who stresses the need to cultivate enactive and ikonic modes of thinking as well as the symbolic mode, or simply the advice of experienced practitioners which has been gathered in the teaching manuals of subject associations or education ministries, the broad consensus is that an abstract concept must be founded on concrete examples and will need sustaining with regular returns to the concrete. The multicultural element does not solve the problem but it can help. For example, whereas we would describe

$$1 + 2 + 3 + \ldots + n$$

as 'the sum of the first n integers', or even as

$$\overset{\text{'} \quad n \quad \text{'}}{\underset{r=1}{\sum} r}$$

the thirteenth-century Chinese mathematician Chu Shih-chieh would call it 'a pile of reeds'. This is no doubt because it can be put in an ikonic form (see Fig. 2.9). A second identical pile can be fitted to this and form a rectangular bundle whose sides are n and $n + 1$ containing $n(n + 1)$ reeds (see Fig. 2.10). So we have shown

$$1 + 2 + 3 + \ldots + n = \tfrac{1}{2}n(n + 1)$$

This liking for concrete examples is typical of Chinese geometry: trapezium, frustum, and tetrahedron were known as 'dustpan-

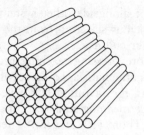

Fig. 2.9. A pile of reeds

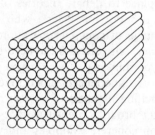

Fig. 2.10. Two piles of reeds

shaped field', 'square pavilion', and 'turtle's shoulder joint'. More-over, the linking of number and algebra to geometric forms is a dominant feature of Greek mathematics. Recently a group of pupils who lacked the necessary algebra to find a formula for

$$1^2 + 2^2 + 3^2 + \ldots + n^2$$

obtained a formula to their satisfaction by constructing six identical pyramids out of plastic cubes and showing they could be fitted together to make a cuboid with edges n, $n + 1$, and $2n + 1$ (see Fig. 2.11). Thus their formula was $\frac{1}{6}n(n + 1)(2n + 1)$.

Negative Aspects

So far we have given positive features of the approach. But there are drawbacks to consider.

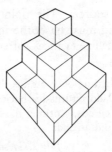

Fig. 2.11. A pyramid of cubes

First, there is the problem of inaccuracy and insecurity. Teachers are used to making mistakes and coping with technical problems in their area of competence—mathematics. But to venture into cultural and historical territory is to live even more dangerously. After a lecture to teachers, I was floored by a questioner who asked why the Pascal triangle (see Fig. 5.5) seemed to be intended to be read lying on its side (for one explanation, see Needham 1959: 137).

A second drawback is that the approach may be misused. A beginner subjected to a plethora of alternative numeral systems may well emerge with the knowledge that other cultures had number systems, but, far from enhancing the pupil's grasp of the decimal system, the experience may have confused and undermined it. The approach can be inappropriate and mistimed.

A third counter-argument runs as follows: 'We now have an efficient, international language of mathematics aided by computers and calculators of awesome power. The child today should move as fast as possible to become conversant and proficient in that language.' To quote Gian-Carlo Rota (1986: 231), 'anything that happened before Leibniz is not history, but palaeontology'. The historical arm of the multicultural approach is then regarded both as irrelevant antiquarianism and, more seriously, as misleading, since certain fundamental elements of modern mathematics are bound to be excluded or at best underemphasized. Elements at risk include the postulational approach, set theory, co-ordinate and vector geometry, probability, and statistics. Of course, a historical approach is possible to such topics but it would depend heavily on European sources. The point about misleading emphasis is important and must be borne in mind. But the charges of 'palaeontology' and 'irrelevance' suffer from the base degrees fallacy.

> BRUTUS. But when he once attains the utmost round,
> He unto the ladder turns his back,
> Looks in the clouds, scorning the base degrees
> By which he did ascend.
>
> *Julius Caesar*, Act II, Scene i

They ignore the parallels between the growth of children's mathematical knowledge and the historical development of mathematics. Moreover, the dream of the more extreme modernists of the post-war era that teaching the formal and abstract language and structures of modern mathematics would best facilitate the young child's progress in mathematics proved an illusion. In its wake we find a move towards a genetic ontology, with teachers striving 'to recreate the fundamental experiences, which from the dawn of historic time, have given rise to mathematical entities' (Thom 1973: 206). Hence, the current emphasis on personal investigations by the pupil, practical work, recreational mathematics, and, we must add, a growing interest in the cultural origins and evolution of the subject.

Teaching Methods

In the next chapter some key topics in elementary mathematics are examined and possible multicultural approaches suggested. It would be unfortunate if this gave the impression that a sequence of lessons on a particular mathematical topic was the only way in which multicultural material might enter the curriculum. Another approach is through personalities, not only the leading figures of the past but contemporary figures like Shakuntula Devi, the world's fastest mental calculator. Great events and popular occasions are another possibility. The four-yearly Olympic games are an obvious source of interesting data. Interdisciplinary work is obviously possible. A study of geometric ornament or rhythm could also involve the art or music department. A study of the mathematics of the Mayas of Central America could be linked to work in history and geography. Finally, a less well-known approach with interesting possibilities is the use of original texts. Here the teacher provides the class with a facsimile text or a translation. An example of this technique is given in Chapter 5. The method has been used extensively with skill and enthusiasm by the M:ATH group in Paris, working with European texts ranging from Euclid's proof that there are infinitely many prime numbers to the announcement in 1904 by von Koch of his Snowflake Curve.

Conclusion

This chapter has discussed the value of a multicultural approach to teaching mathematics, its strengths, its limitations, and ways in which it might be implemented. In conclusion it would seem that the approach should be used sensitively and judiciously, the teacher striking a balance between personal interest and the constraints of the external curriculum. For, if the approach is used, it must enhance rather than retard the child's progress.

Our task then is to seek out, on the one hand, cultural materials which offer mathematical gains, and, on the other, mathematical activities which make an effective contribution to multicultural education.

These twin objectives are the driving force behind the following chapter, which studies some of the key elements of the mathematics curriculum.

3 Ten Key Areas of the Curriculum

DAVID NELSON

In this chapter we take ten key content areas likely to be studied by all schoolchildren, whatever their ability, and look at them from a multicultural point of view. They are:

- number
- money
- percentages
- use of calculator
- time
- measurement
- graphs and pictorial representation
- spatial concepts
- ratio and proportion
- statistical ideas

The aim is to alert and inform the reader of some of the possibilities and thus encourage further enquiry in these and other areas. Lack of space precludes any attempt at comprehensive treatment, but in any case that would be foreign to the enterprise, since it is hoped that the reader will enjoy finding and sharing new materials.

We did consider alternative methods of presentation and organization. Another approach would have been to link materials to certain key processes in mathematics; a list of activities might have included:

- counting and calculating
- drawing and measuring
- playing
- guessing and proving

In fact we decided to adopt an approach linking materials to certain key areas of the *content* of mathematics; the list of areas is taken from the Cockcroft Report (DES 1982) on mathematics education in England and Wales, where it was proposed, and later found general acceptance, as a foundation list for study by all secondary pupils. The existence of such a relatively uncontroversial common core was one reason for favouring an approach by content areas. Another was the tendency amongst the general public and educators (as exemplified by the above list) to think of mathematics more in terms of specific content than of general processes and activities.

The topic areas are, of course, neither independent nor exclusive. For example, a study of ratio and proportion will involve number concepts and calculation and maybe spatial concepts and measurement. Conversely, a study of money will at some stage involve conversion from one currency to another—an exercise in proportion (or the use of graphs).

The materials that follow must *not* be seen as prescriptive. They are put forward as suggestions which have some mathematical merit. But no more. In arriving at a proper educational programme for an individual or a class, the professional teacher examines potential sources of material and then selects or constructs suitable material and a method of delivery appropriate to the situation. Our aim is simply to introduce another potential source worthy of exploration.

Nor is any special guidance on teaching method necessary. The modern teacher is trained to do much more than follow a programme of work contained in a series of textbooks or commercial learning schemes. The ability to devise appropriate learning materials and situations is also essential. So also is the ability to guide pupils in investigative work and personal or group project work.

Nor do we prescribe the ages or abilities of pupils who might benefit from the materials. This, too, is a matter for the professional judgement of the teacher. Moreover, much of the material can be used at various stages, ranging from the early formative years to later more advanced stages, when there is a need to reflect on concepts and develop an overview of the subject. In practice we have found it possible to adapt items, and Chapter 5 shows an idea adapted for use with elementary and advanced pupils.

Table 3.1. A table compiled after the 1988 Olympic Games in Seoul

	Position in final medal table	No. of medals	Population per medal (000,000)
East Germany	2	102	0.167
New Zealand	18	13	0.231
Bulgaria	7	35	0.258
Hungary	6	23	0.479
Sweden	32	11	0.728
Norway	21	5	0.800
Romania	8	24	0.959
Jamaica	34	2	1.000
Australia	15	14	1.143
South Korea	4	33	1.243
Denmark	23	4	1.250
Finland	25	4	1.250
West Germany	5	40	1.525
Netherlands	22	9	1.667
Yugoslavia	16	12	1.917
Czechoslovakia	17	8	2.000
USSR	1	132	2.129
Kenya	13	9	2.334
Britain	12	24	2.375
Poland	20	16	2.375
Canada	19	10	2.600
USA	3	94	2.649
France	9	16	3.438
Italy	10	14	4.072
Japan	14	14	8.643
Spain	26	4	9.750
Brazil	24	6	23.000
China	11	28	37.643

Source: 'When size and wealth are not everything', *Independent*, 4 Oct. 1988.

Finally, and here we run the risk of seeming prescriptive, we emphasize the value of 'informed opportunism' on the part of the teacher—the art of building on the 'conversation' between pupil(s) and teacher. Consider, for example, Table 3.1. How might this appear in the classroom? It could follow the announcement 'today's topic is statistical tables'. But it could also follow the commonly made observation that success in international sport does not necessarily reflect the size of a nation's population or its wealth.

We now present our materials grouped under the content areas listed at the beginning of the chapter. With usually three or more illustrative examples or classroom problems per topic, considera-

Table 3.2. Number words in various languages

English	Italian	German	Greek	Sanskrit
one	uno	eins	heis	ekab
two	due	zwei	dyo	dvi
three	tre	drei	treis	trayah
four	quattro	vier	tettares	catvarah
five	cinque	fünf	pente	panca

Table 3.3. Examples of '2-count'

Number	Gumugal (Australia)	Bakairi (Central Brazil)	Bushman (Southern Africa)
1	urapon	tokale	xa
2	ukasar	ahage	t'oa
3	ukasar-urapon	ahage tokale	'quo
4	ukasar-ukasar	ahage ahage	t'oa t'oa

tions of space call for a fairly terse presentation. In each case we hope to give sufficient information for the reader to go on to judge its classroom potential.

Number

This area is, of course, rich in possibilities. We have collected our selection of examples and suggestions under five headings:

- counting
- written numerals
- number systems
- magic squares
- square roots

Counting

Modern counting is almost universally ten-based and it is interesting to compare the words used for numbers in some cultures (see Table 3.2). But there are cultures in which counting is based more or less on just two words (those for one and two). This phenomenon is known as '2-count' (see Table 3.3). The books by Flegg

Table 3.4. Number words for 1–21 in Gujerati, Welsh, and Yoruba

No.	Gujerati	Welsh*	Yoruba
1	ek	un	ookan
2	tho	dau (dwy)	eeji
3	teen	tri (tair)	eeta
4	char	pedwar (pedair)	eerin
5	panch	pump	aarun
6	chez	chwech	eefa
7	saat	saith	eeje
8	aat	wyth	eejo
9	now	naw	eesan
10	dus	deg	eewaa
11	agiyar	un ar ddeg	ookanlaa
12	bar	deuddeg	eejilaa
13	ter	tri (tair) ar ddeg	eetalaa
14	chowd	pedwar (pedair) ar ddeg	eerinlaa
15	pandhar	pymtheg	aarundinlogun
16	sol	un ar bymtheg	eerindinlogun
17	sattar	dau (dwy) ar bymtheg	eetadinlogun
18	adhar	tri (tair) ar bymtheg	eejidinlogun
19	ognwyss	pedwar (pedair) ar bymtheg	ookandinlogun
20	wyss	ugain	ogun
21	ekwyss	un ar hugain	ookanlelogun

* The words in brackets are feminine forms.

(1983, 1989), Ifrah (1985), and Menninger (1969) are excellent sources of material on counting, numerals, and number systems.

It is possible that a better understanding of our own language of counting can be obtained by asking a class to listen to sounds and rhythms of another counting system and to note its irregularities and differences from our system. The words used for counting usually show the basic groupings and the ways of building increasingly high numbers.*

To illustrate, consider the language of counting in (1) Gujerati, a regional language of India, (2) Welsh, a minority language of the British Isles, and (3) Yoruba, a regional language of West Africa. An examination of Table 3.4 shows that the 'units' sound invari-

---

* In a classroom fortunate enough to have a diversity of languages, children should be called upon to count in languages that they know. This is not only sound educational practice, but an encouragement for children to learn more than one language.

ably precedes the 'tens' sound in both Welsh and Yoruba. For example, in Yoruba 13 is *eetalaa*, *eeta* being the word for 3. In Gujerati, 13 is known as *ter*, which is a derivative of the word for 3 (*teen*). Indeed, the words for 11–18 in Gujerati are all derived from the corresponding words for the numbers 1–8. In Welsh after 15 a convention occurs which is found in no other European language. The words for 16, 17, 18, and 19 are formed by adding units on to 15 (*pymtheg*). Thus the feminine form of 19 is *pedair ar bymtheg*: *pedair* (4) *ar* (+) *bymtheg* (15). A 'subtraction' principle may be observed in both Gujerati and Yoruba; numbers above 10 ending in 9 are counted as 'one less than' the successive number. Thus in Gujerati, 19 is *ognwyss* or 'one less than *wyss* (20)'; 29 is *ogntryss* or 'one less than *tryss*' (30) (see Table 3.4).

At another level of counting and number representation there are different mechanical aids, such as the Chinese rods, the Inca quipu, and the Japanese soroban (see Chapter 4). However, the most accessible of the mechanical aids for representational purposes remains our fingers. It is possible, using each hand, to devise different systems such as counting finger tips (1–5) or counting finger joints (1–15). A more complex system was used in ancient China, in which each of the three faces of each of the finger joints of each finger was allocated a number from 1 to 9. When all five fingers of a hand were brought into play, each successive finger indicating increasing powers of 10, the hand offered a highly economical way of representing numbers up to 10^5 (see Fig. 3.1). With both hands, it became possible to add, subtract, and even multiply a pair of numbers. This surely represents a triumph of mind over technology!

Written Numerals

When encouraging children to develop consistent and well-formed written numerals (mathematical handwriting as it were), it can be useful to introduce some of the ancestors of our modern numerals. This creates an interest in the numerals as objects, while comparisons of forms involve geometric ideas such as reflection and rotation (see Fig. 3.2).

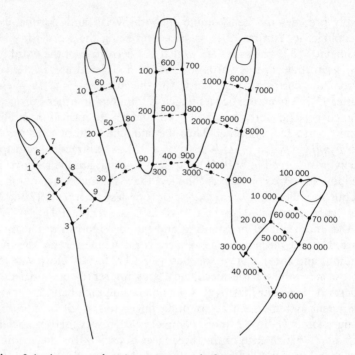

Fig. 3.1. A comprehensive system of finger-counting from China (Hemmings 1984: 117)

Number Systems

The Mayans and Babylonians had number systems based on 20 and 60 respectively. A system which comes closer to the decimal Hindu–Arabic system is the old Chinese rod numeral system. This is a positional place value system with base 10 but uses two sets of numerals—one for the units, hundreds, ten thousands, etc., and the other for the tens, thousands, etc. (see Fig. 3.3). Thus 1346 would be written

$$- \quad ||| \quad \equiv \quad \top$$

An instance of its use in the classroom is given in Chapter 5.
For experience of a different type, the simple grouping system

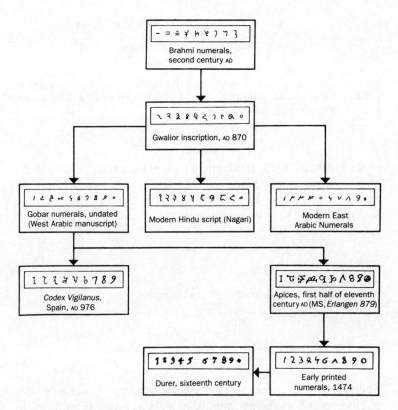

Fig. 3.2. Family tree of Hindu–Arabic numerals (Open University 1976: 53)

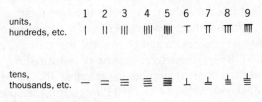

	1	2	3	4	5	6	7	8	9
units, hundreds, etc.	I	II	III	IIII	IIIII	T	TT	TTT	TTTT

| tens, thousands, etc. | — | = | ≡ | ≡ | ≡ | ⊥ | ⊥ | ⊥ | ⊥ |

Fig. 3.3. Chinese rod numerals

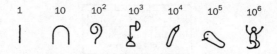

Fig. 3.4. Hieroglyphs used in an Egyptian numeral system; from left to right: vertical stroke, heelbone, coil of rope, lotus flower, bent finger, burbot fish, kneeling figure

of the Egyptians—a hieroglyphic numeral system based on powers of 10—seems best (see Fig. 3.4). The system is unambiguous, does not use a zero, and the symbols can be written in any order, so that, whereas 143 was usually written

III ∩∩∩∩ ⁹

no confusion would arise if it was written

⁹ ∩∩∩∩ III

Addition of 143 and 211 in this system places a similar emphasis on 'like terms', as the addition of $x^2 + 4x + 3$ and $2x^2 + x + 1$ in algebra.

Magic Squares

Magic squares seem to have originated a long time ago in China, and the Lo Shu is a good starting-point for investigating them (see Fig. 3.5). The subsequent development and widespread occurrence of magic squares makes them a good topic for multicultural study. Rouse Ball (1892) is a useful source of information on magic squares and their construction by, for example, the 'Knight's move' method. Zaslavsky (1973) gives an interesting account of the work of the eighteenth-century West African Muhammad ibn Muhammad.

Needham (1959: 60) gives a Japanese magic cube from Pi Nai's

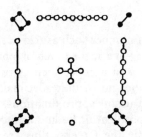

Fig. 3.5. The earliest recorded magic square: the Lo Shu (Needham 1959: 57)

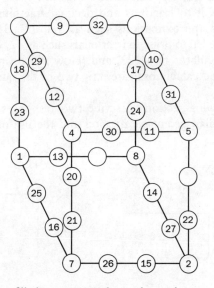

Fig. 3.6. Can you fill the empty circles with numbers so as to make a magic cube? (derived from Needham 1959: 60)

nineteenth-century 'Mountain Hut Records'. If some numbers are erased, as in Fig. 3.6, the problem of filling in the missing numbers not only makes an interesting puzzle for classroom use but can lead to an investigation of ways of extending the idea of a magic square to three dimensions.

Square Roots

The square root of a number such as 625 is either known by heart or found to be twenty-five at the touch of a button on a calculator. But the square root of a number such as two is certainly not an integer, nor a fraction, nor a finite decimal, even though $1\frac{2}{5}$ and 1.414 are good and useful approximations.

Historically, the problem of finding a fraction equal to $\sqrt{2}$ was proved impossible by the Greeks, thus creating a new class of numbers—the non-rationals or *irrationals*—which were not integers nor fractions.

Educationally, the development of the concept of number follows a similar pattern. The child builds a scheme of integers and then extends it to fractions and decimal fractions. Though they first enter as approximations such as 1.4, 1.7, $3\frac{1}{7}$, a further extension is needed to bring in irrationals such as $\sqrt{2}$, $\sqrt{3}$, π, etc. 'How does my calculator find $\sqrt{2}$?' and 'How did people calculate $\sqrt{2}$ before we had calculators? are only two of the questions children ask.

The following sections describe two responses to these questions: an Indian geometric method and the use of iterative techniques.

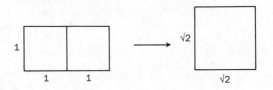

Fig. 3.7

Geometric method

Baudhayana's *Sulbasutra* (*c*.800–500 BC) seems to have put the problem in geometrical form: 'Convert two unit squares into a square of area 2 (and therefore side $\sqrt{2}$)' (see Fig. 3.7). The first steps, beginning by dividing one square into thirds, can be illustrated diagrammatically (see Fig. 3.8), showing that

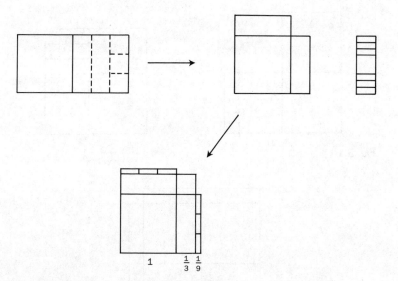

Fig. 3.8

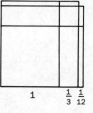

Fig. 3.9

$$1\tfrac{1}{3} < \sqrt{2} < 1 + \tfrac{1}{3} + \tfrac{1}{9}$$

The next step is to shave off two strips of width $\tfrac{1}{36}$ and redistribute them, so that (Fig. 3.9)

$$\sqrt{2} \simeq 1 + \tfrac{1}{3} + \tfrac{1}{12}$$
$$= 1.41\dot{6}$$

and so on. Joseph (1991) gives further approximations.

Other square roots can be approximated to in this intuitive

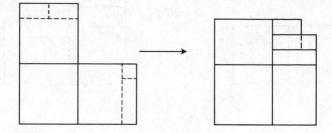

Fig. 3.10

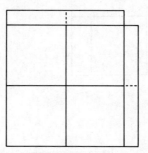

Fig. 3.11

geometric way. The reorganization of three squares illustrated in Fig. 3.10 shows that

$$1\tfrac{1}{2} < \sqrt{3} < 1\tfrac{3}{4}$$

while the rearrangement of five squares in Fig. 3.11 shows that

$$2 < \sqrt{5} < 2\tfrac{1}{4}$$

We can continue the exploration into three dimensions and try, for example, to combine two unit cubes into a single cube of volume 2 cubic units and side $\sqrt[3]{2}$. A possible first stage is illustrated in Fig. 3.12. By adding pieces on to the left-hand cube we have made a cube with side $1\tfrac{1}{4}$, and have a tower of three $\tfrac{1}{4} \times \tfrac{1}{4} \times \tfrac{1}{4}$ cubes still to be used. If each little cube is sliced horizontally into twenty-five equal slices, these can be used to cover the top, front, and a side face of the largest cube and turn it almost into a cube with side $1\tfrac{1}{4} + \tfrac{1}{100}$. We conclude that

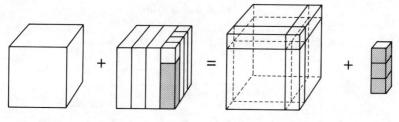

Fig. 3.12

$$1\tfrac{1}{4} < \sqrt[3]{2} < 1\tfrac{1}{4} + \tfrac{1}{100}$$

i.e. $\qquad 1.25 < \sqrt[3]{2} < 1.26$

In fact, $\sqrt[3]{2}$ = 1.2599 to four decimal places, so, in two stages, we have come very close to success. The *Sulbasutra* construction for $\sqrt{2}$ is a good example of a piece of 'cultural' mathematics acting as a starting-point for creative and valuable investigations by children. Among the virtues of the investigation are:

- the value of giving the root a geometric (concrete) form,
- the interplay between geometry and arithmetic,
- the dissection and rearrangement of shapes,
- the use of inequalities,
- obtaining better and better approximations to an unknown quantity,
- showing that this geometric approach can be continued in three dimensions but no further,
- showing that the eight parts of the largest cube in Fig. 3.12 illustrate the algebraic identity

$$(a + b)^3 = a^3 + 3a^2b + 3ab^2 + b^3$$

with $a = 1$ and $b = \tfrac{1}{4}$.

Iterative methods

In my experience, of the two iterative techniques, young children seem less interested in Hero of Alexandria's (fl. AD 62) algorithm for the square root of N, even though their calculators probably use it, than in the old 'division method' for square roots.

Hero's method, illustrated in Fig. 3.13, is easy and fast. Going for $\sqrt{2}$ with 1 as a first guess we get

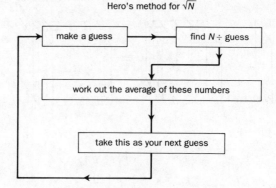

Fig. 3.13. Hero's method for calculating $\sqrt{N}$

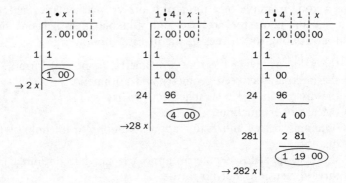

Fig. 3.14. Extracting $\sqrt{2}$ by a 'division method'

$$1, 1.5, 1.416, 1.41421568628 \ldots$$

and the first five decimal places of the last number are already correct.

The 'division method', or methods very similar to it, is found in the early stages of the development of mathematics in various cultures: Greek, Indian, Arabian, Chinese, and possibly Babylonian. The first stages in calculating $\sqrt{2}$ are shown in Fig. 3.14. The method is iterative in the sense that it is repetitive and each stage provides input for the next stage. The calculation of the digit marked x in each diagram is interesting and calls for either pencil and paper or a mixture of estimation and mental arithmetic. The digit x is chosen so that its product with the arrowed number is as close to but not greater than the ringed number. (The arrowed number is created by doubling the digits in the top line and placing x in the unit position.) Unlike Hero's method it is slow and tedious, but it has the advantage of being exact, in the sense that every answer digit produced is correct and so the decimal $\sqrt{2}$ is slowly revealed digit by digit. This exact procession of digits, together with the curious calculation of x, perhaps account for its appeal.

Older pupils may be able to find an algebraic justification for the method. A similar, more complex, method for cube roots was widespread and details can be found in Flegg (1983). Hero's method can also be adapted to find cube roots and, again, some pupils may be able to find this adjustment for themselves.

Money

National currencies and exchange of money is an obvious area for exploration. Modern textbooks rarely stray beyond a few European and North American currencies. Not so Samuel Young, Master of the Academy, Princess Street, Manchester, who, in his *Practical Arithmetic* of 1864, informs his reader of the currencies of over thirty countries or provinces ranging from Jamaica to Calcutta. In the following brief extract (1864: 127) note that £1 sterling = 240d. in Britain before 1971.

XVIII. SWEDEN AND NORWAY.

<table>
<tr><td>Stockholm.</td><td>Christiani.</td></tr>
<tr><td>48 skillings = 1 rix dollar.</td><td>96 skillings = 1 specie dollar.</td></tr>
</table>

Exchange Stockholm with Britain. 11 rix dollars, 24 skillings, for £1.
Exchange Christiani with Britain. 6 specie dollars, 24 skillings, for £1.

XIX. TURKEY, CONSTANTINOPLE. EGYPT, ALEXANDRIA.

40 paras = 1 piastre.

The value of the piastre is about 4d. at Constantinople, and $3\frac{1}{5}d$. at Alexandria.

Exchange Constantinople with Britain. $58\frac{1}{2}$ piastres for £1.

Bills on London are usually drawn at 61 days' sight, and on all other places at 31 days' sight.

Young's range of currencies, rather than reflecting idealistic internationalism, is surely a product of his aim to provide applications of the rules of arithmetic to 'Mercantile, Cotton Spinning, Manufacturing and Mechanical Calculations' and the busy manufacturing and trading environment in which he worked.

Apart from widening the range of countries discussed, the modern teacher has other avenues open. Some pupils may have experience, actual or through relatives, of life in another country—in particular its currency and comparative cost of living. Others may have visited other countries briefly on holiday and thus bring first-hand data on exchange rates and costs to the classroom. Information from travel agents can be used to plan and budget for future holidays (real or imaginary). These plans can take time zones into account (see International Time, p. 67). Another approach is through stamps. It is, of course, helpful if any pupils are stamp collectors. But at the simplest level an airmail letter from, say, Japan can lead to discussion of Japanese currency, conversion of the Japanese postal charge to sterling, and a comparison with the cost of sending such a letter from Britain to Japan. In January 1989 the costs were

Japan to Britain	120 yen
Britain to Japan	37 pence
Exchange rate £1 = 240 yen	

The figures for South Korea were

South Korea to Britain	400 won
Britain to South Korea	37 pence
Exchange Rate £1 = 1,100 won	

Over a short period a group of children could obtain and tabulate comparisons for a wide range of countries.

In her book *Africa Counts* Claudia Zaslavsky (1973) refers to the once widespread use of cowrie shells as currency in many parts of Africa. An interdisciplinary project on history and geography could include the cowrie-shell currency, its exploitation and its downfall. Use could be made of tables such as the following, which was in operation at the beginning of the century in Buganda:

1 cow	= 2,500 cowries
1 male slave	= 1 cow
1 female slave	= 4 or 5 cows
5 goats	= 1 cow
1 ivory tusk	= 1,000 cowries

Percentages

Mathematics lessons in secondary schools are very often not about anything. You collect like terms, or learn the laws of indices, with no perception of why anyone needs to do such things. There is excessive preoccupation with a sequence of skills and quite inadequate opportunity to see the skills emerging from the solution of problems. As a consequence of this approach, school mathematics contains very little incidental information. A French lesson might well contain incidental information about France—so on across the curriculum; but in mathematics the incidental information you might expect (current exchange and interest rates; general knowledge on climate, communications and geography; the rules and scoring systems of games; social statistics) is rarely there, because most teachers in no way see this as part of their responsibility when teaching mathematics.

(DES 1982: 141–2)

Table 3.5 provides information about British society and requires an understanding of percentages for its appreciation. It is taken from *Key Data 1986*, a small selection of statistics produced annually by the Central Statistical Office and intended for general readership. In the body of the table, numbers in italic represent percentages and numbers in roman represent raw figures. At first sight the table appears straightforward, easy to understand, and of considerable value in giving children an indication of the numerical strengths of various ethnic groups. Indeed it would be natural for an Indian pupil to calculate what percentage of the UK population are Indian. What guidance might pupils need in appreciating these statistics and reconciling them with their view of the society in which they live?

1. A minor difficulty, which may disconcert some, is that, due to rounding, the percentages in some rows (e.g. African, Arab) do not sum to 100.

Table 3.5. Population of Great Britain, by ethnic origin and age, 1983

	Age				Total all ages (000)
	0–15 (%)	16–29 (%)	30–44 (%)	45 or over (%)	
Ethnic origin					
White	21	21	20	38	50,798
West Indian or Guyanese	25	34	19	22	503
Indian	33	27	23	17	791
Pakistani	45	24	18	13	355
Bangladeshi	54	18	16	12	81
Chinese	30	32	26	13	106
African	30	30	26	13	91
Arab	21	39	26	15	69
Mixed	54	26	11	9	196
Other	26	24	37	13	109
Not stated	35	21	15	29	879
All origins	22	21	20	37	53,979

Source: Central Statistical Office (1986: Table 2.4, p. 9).

2. The percentage representations for some groups are less than 1 per cent. The table gives 91,000 Africans in a population of about 54 million. As a percentage this is 0.2 per cent and it may be necessary to discard the 100 point scale of reference and express this as '2 in 1,000'. Even then, can we be sure the pupil can imagine such a level of representation unaided?

3. The origin of 879,000 people is given as 'not stated'. To which groups do they belong? If they were *proportionately* drawn from the ethnic groups, only 52,000 would come from the minority groups, so only slight changes in their totals would be needed. Until one consults the full survey and finds it suggested that this *was* the case, the figure of 879,000 has a disturbing effect. Interestingly, the numbers of 'not stated' have fallen steadily from 879,000 in 1983 to 46,000 in 1987.

4. It is well known that the minority groups are not evenly distributed geographically and in some areas are highly concentrated. (In 1987, for example, whereas the ethnic minorities constituted 4.5 per cent of the entire population they were 9.7 per cent of the population in the metropolitan counties.) On the basis of Table 3.5, there are, in general, 15

Table 3.6. African, Bangladeshi, and Indian populations in Great Britain, 1983–7 (000s)

Ethnic group	Year					Average 1985–7
	1983	1984	1985	1986	1987	
African	91	109	102	98	116	105
Bangladeshi	81	93	99	117	116	110
Indian	791	807	689	784	761	745

Source: Compiled from Office of Population Censuses and Surveys (1987–9).

Indians per 1,000 population and, allowing for the percentage in the 0–15 age group, 22 Indian children per 1,000 under 16. But both these proportions may well be greatly at odds with a pupil's experience, and informed support from the teacher is needed.

In the *Labour Force Surveys* of 1985, 1986, and 1987 (Office of Population Censuses and Surveys 1987–9) the tables are based on an annual survey of about 60,000 households, in which the heads of households were 'asked to which ethnic group they and members of their household belong'. Though allowance is made for the uneven geographical distribution of the ethnic minorities, such annual estimates are subject to large sampling errors. Table 3.6 gives estimates of African, Bangladeshi, and Indian populations for 1983–7. Because of these variations, later surveys issued a table giving a three-year average rather than an estimate for a single year.

Since the ethnic composition of a school and local community may differ considerably from the overall picture for the country, it might be helpful to obtain and discuss figures for the town, city, or region in which the school lies. But once again informed guidance from the teacher will be necessary.

It is worth noting that 'percentage' is an idea which is not culture free. Reducing all fractions and proportions to a 100-point scale presumes a decimal number system. Curiously one of the earliest problems on compound interest comes from the Louvre tablet of 1700 BC, which asks, in modern terms, how long it takes for a sum of money to double in value if interest is compounded at 20 per cent per annum. But this is a Babylonian tablet and the interest rate is expressed as '12 per 60', since their number system was sexagesimal. Incidentally, the Babylonian answer of

$$3 + \frac{47}{60} + \frac{13}{60^2} + \frac{20}{60^3} \text{ years}$$

suggests it may have been obtained by a linear approximation (interpolation) based on the values of the investment after three and four years.

Use of calculator

Most educators agree it is essential to cultivate three modes of calculation—mental, on paper, and with a calculator. Here we make four suggestions for classroom work which provide exercise in all three modes, with the calculator usually leading but sometimes supporting.

Vedic Multiplication

Vedic multiplication is still taught in India and is discussed in detail in Chapter 4. Here is a simple example written out in full:

$$
\begin{array}{r}
65 \\
\times 23 \\
\hline
1495 \\
\hline
\scriptstyle 21
\end{array}
$$

and here is the underlying mental calculation:

$$5 \times 3 = 15, \text{ write 5, carry 1}$$
$$6 \times 3 + 2 \times 5 + 1 = 29, \text{ write 9, carry 2}$$
$$6 \times 2 + 2 = 14, \text{ write 14}$$

The method involves less paperwork than 'long multiplication' and is easily mastered. Children enjoy turning the algorithm into geometrical form, finding methods for larger numbers, trying to explain the method, and, of course, checking their answers on their calculators.

Short cuts for squares and square roots

A method found in the *Brahmasphuta siddhanta* of the seventh century Indian Brahmagupta and used by some 'lightning' mental calculators to square numbers goes as follows:

$$889^2 = 878 \times 900 + 11^2$$
$$= 790\ 321$$

It is based on the fact that

$$a^2 = (a - b)(a + b) + b^2$$

the trick being to make $a + b$ (or $a - b$) a multiple of 100. To begin with, try 999^2 and 512^2 this way.

When squaring three-digit numbers mentally, one needs squares up to 49, but these can in turn be found the same way:

$$843^3 = 800 \times 886 + 43^2$$
$$= 708\ 800 + 40 \times 46 + 3^2$$
$$= 708\ 800 + 1840 + 9$$
$$= 710\ 649$$

Turning to square roots, a method of estimating known to the Egyptians (Cairo papyrus) and the Babylonians is based on the approximation:

$$\sqrt{a^2 + b} \simeq a + \frac{b}{2a}$$

For example,

since
$$17 = 4^2 + 1$$
$$\sqrt{17} \simeq 4 + \frac{1}{2 \times 4}$$
$$= 4.125$$

the true value being $4.123\ldots$

The number b can be negative in value:

since
$$23 = 5^2 - 2$$
$$\sqrt{23} \simeq 5 - \frac{2}{2 \times 5}$$
$$= 4.8$$

the true value being $4.7958\ldots$

All these shortcuts encourage the use of algebra or geometry to justify the methods and perhaps to extend them to cubes or to cube roots. They involve the calculator to check the results or to test predictions.

Plimpton 322

A worksheet such as Fig. 3.15 can introduce children to calculator-aided detective work on one of the mysteries of the extraordinary Babylonian tablet known as Plimpton 322. This could be supported by a picture of the original tablet (see Eves 1990; Neugebauer 1962). If a hint is needed, one theory is that the tablet was a 'teacher's aid for setting up and solving problems involving right triangles' (Friberg 1981: 302).

Inversion

Finally we give an example where the calculator is used to help solve certain types of algebraic problems. To introduce it, consider the conversion of a Fahrenheit temperature to a Celsius temperature:

subtract 32, multiply by 5, and divide by 9

Thus 212 °F converts to 100 °C. If, on the other hand, we are given a Celsius temperature, say 60 °C, then the problem of finding the Fahrenheit equivalent F is that of solving the equation

$$(F - 32) \times \tfrac{5}{9} = 60$$

and this can be done on the calculator by reversing and inverting the rule for conversion. Thus, having entered 60, the key strokes are:

multiply by 9, divide by 5, and add 32

Though the method applies only to equations which can be written in a form where the unknown only occurs once, the technique has enjoyed a revival in schools recently. The method was known to the early Indian mathematicians as *inversion*. Here is Aryabhata's definition in his *Aryabhatiya* (c. AD 499): 'Multiplication becomes

Plimpton 322

Can you solve the mystery of this Babylonian tablet? (−1900 < t < −1600) Four errors (in brackets) have been corrected by modern scholars. The error in line 9 is easy to make if you remember that originally all the numbers were written to base 60. The error in line 13 is revealing.

119	169	1
3367	4825 [11521]	2
4601	6649	3
12709	18541	4
65	97	5
319	481	6
2291	3541	7
799	1249	8
481 [541]	769	9
4961	8161	10
45	75	11
1679	2929	12
161 [25921]	289	13
1771	3229	14
56	106 [53]	15

Fig. 3.15. Plimpton 322: a worksheet for a classroom investigation

division, division becomes multiplication; what was gain becomes loss, what was loss, gain; inversion'. This is one of his problems:

Beautiful maiden with beaming eyes, tell me, as thou understandest the method of inversion, which is the number which multiplied by 3, then increased by $\frac{3}{4}$ of the product, then divided by 7, diminished by $\frac{1}{3}$ of the quotient, multiplied by itself, diminished by 52, by the extraction of the square root, addition of 8, and division by 10 gives the number 2?

Time

A typical school programme does little more than cover the units of time measurement, the 24-hour clock, and the reading of timetables. Cultural considerations are invariably neglected and the work is usually undemanding. This need not be the case. For example, the sketch in Fig. 3.16 could be used to introduce contemporary French culture and some careful calculator work. This

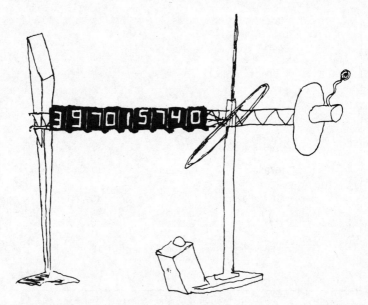

Fig. 3.16. The gantry near the Pompidou Centre in Paris reading 397015740 at 11.45 on 2 June 1987; the nine-figure number is decreasing by one unit every second

drawing depicts an unusual construction standing outside the Pompidou Centre in Paris. The dials on the gantry show a nine-figure number and every second the number goes down one unit. The dials read 397015740 at 11.45 on 2 June 1987, so one second later the reading was 397015739. A challenging classroom activity, with children probably working in small groups, is to find out the time and date when the dials register 000000000.

We suggest three areas for exploration in this topic.

International Time

The increase in global travel and communications makes international time a suitable theme for schoolwork. Using travel brochures and telephone directories, planning real or imaginary foreign itineraries, and timing and costing telephone calls which take into account time zones and charge bands, provide useful exercises in arithmetic. In addition, the financial planning will involve foreign currencies (see Money, p. 58).

Dates of Festivals

Classroom activity suggested earlier in this section called on knowledge of the Gregorian calendar of 365 days with an extra day in every year whose number is divisible by 4 except for centenary years which are not divisible by 400.

There are other complexities. Certain festivals such as Christmas Day fall on fixed days. Some do not. The Christian festival of Easter falls on the Sunday which follows the first full moon after the vernal equinox (about 21 March). Its date determines those of other festivals, such as Shrove Tuesday and Whit Sunday, and affects the length of the spring term in schools. Other important festivals and events include the Chinese New Year, the Jewish feasts of Passover and Yom Kippur, and the Muslim thirty-day Ramadan in the ninth month of the Muslim Year.

Types of Calendar

Calculating the dates of festivals will probably involve knowing the structure of the underlying calendar. We have already alluded to the Chinese, Jewish, and Muslim calendars and this would seem a fruitful area for collaboration between teachers of Mathematics and Religious Studies. Having explored different types of calendar and numbering of years (for example, the Jewish New Year 5750 and the Muslim New Year 1410 fell in 1989), mention might be made of the widespread use in primitive societies of *phenomenon* calendars. In a phenomenon calendar our metrical, abstract concept of time is largely absent, and is replaced by a day ordered by events such as 'sunrise', a 'week' of from three to eight days which suits the cycle of work and markets in the locality, and a 'year' of variable length which is not completed until its major seasons are complete.

This topic seems ideal for interdisciplinary work in which the mathematical content is less important than the cultural and religious. Nevertheless, the arithmetic involved requires careful calculation and organization. For example, in the case of the Jewish calendar, years are solar but vary slightly in length and are numbered from 3761 BC. Each year contains twelve lunar months of thirty or twenty-nine days with a thirteenth month of thirty days intercalated every third, sixth, eighth, eleventh, fourteenth, seventeenth, and nineteenth year of a nineteen-year cycle. In the case of the Muslim calendar, years are numbered from the Hegira of AD 622 (Muhammad's emigration from Mecca to Medina). Each year contains twelve lunar months of thirty and twenty-nine days alternately, giving 354 days in all. In eleven of the years in a thirty-year cycle an extra day is intercalated. So in this calendar the months regress through all the seasons in about thirty-three years. Stern and Nejad (1991: 14) give an algorithm for converting from the Muslim calendar to the Gregorian calendar.

Measurement

We begin this section by describing two events in history which a teacher could use to enrich this topic, and close with some details of attempts to measure π.

Our first event is a remarkable application of mathematics to estimate the circumference of the earth. It was the work of Eratosthenes (*c*.275–194 BC) at Alexandria in Egypt (*c*.230 BC). The

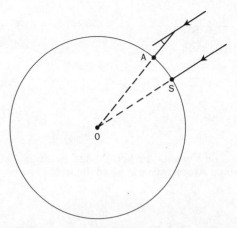

Fig. 3.17. The basis for Eratosthenes' determination of the circumference of the earth; when the sun was overhead at Syene (S), its rays made an angle of $7\frac{1}{5}°$ with the vertical at Alexandria (A), 5000 stades due north of Syene

basis was the observation that at midday on the summer solstice the sun was directly overhead at Syene (near Aswan), while at Alexandria the sun's rays made an angle of $7\frac{1}{5}°$ with the vertical (see Fig. 3.17). Estimating the distance between Syene and Alexandria to be 5000 stades and believing the two places to lie on the same meridian, Eratosthenes estimated the circumference of the earth to be 250 000 stades, later adding 2000 stades to give a number divisible by 60. The exact size of the stade is unknown: one estimate is 559 feet (170 metres). Syene lies close to the Tropic of Cancer, but this is not essential to attempts to re-enact this event. If two schools on the same meridian in, say, Dundee (3°W, 56.5°N) and Newport (3°W, 51.6°N) were to measure the angle of the sun's rays made with the vertical at midday on the same day, the difference between these angles and the distance between Dundee and Newport would provide the basis for the calculation.

Our second event is a striking instance of the effect a small error can have on a calculation. The Greek mathematician Aristarchus of Samos (*c*.310–*c*.230 BC)—the first heliocentrist and thus the 'Copernicus of antiquity'—tried to estimate the relative distances of the sun and moon from the earth. At half-moon (see Fig. 3.18)

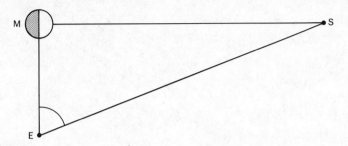

Fig. 3.18. Diagram showing the Sun (S) and Earth (E), with the moon (M) at half-moon; Aristarchus estimated angle MES to be $\frac{29}{30}$ of a right angle (87°)

he estimated angle MES to be $\frac{29}{30}$ of a right angle. He correctly deduced the ratio SE : ME to be between 18 : 1 and 20 : 1. However, his estimate of the angle was 2°50′ too small and his estimate of the ratio is very inaccurate. With the aid of modern trigonometry and astronomy we see that an error of 3 per cent in angle MES is responsible for the ratio being eighteen times too small!

Finally, the measurement of π has occupied mathematicians of many cultures and is a good theme for schoolwork at any secondary level. Eves (1990) and Smith (1923–5) are easily accessible sources of material. However, to give an impression of the range of cultures involved we give a few of the approximations in Table 3.7.

Graphs and pictorial representation

In the earlier section on percentages the discussion of data on the ethnic origins of the British population (see Table 3.5) was conducted in verbal–numerical terms. It is possible to give this quantitative information a visual representation and, using the given data, one can produce bar charts, pictograms, pie charts, and time series. Fig. 3.19 is a double bar chart comparing the age structures of two groups.

The cultivation of graphical integrity—faithful representation and good design—is an important aim. We need a critical ap-

Table 3.7. Approximations of π

Source	Mathematician	Approximation
Old Testament (1 Kgs. 7: 23; 2 Chr. 4: 2)	—	3
Babylonian	—	$\frac{25}{8}$
Egyptian	—	$\frac{256}{81}$
Greek	Archimedes (240 BC)	$3\frac{10}{71} < \pi < 3\frac{1}{7}$
	Ptolemy (150 AD)	$3 + \frac{8}{60} + \frac{30}{3600}$
Chinese	Liu Hui (c.263 AD)	3.1416
	Tsu Chung Chi (fifth century AD)	$\begin{cases} 3.1415926 < \pi < 3.1415927 \\ \frac{355}{113} \end{cases}$
Indian	Aryabhata (c.530 AD)	$\frac{62832}{20000}$
	Bhaskara (c.1150 AD)	$\frac{3927}{1250}$ and $\sqrt{10}$
Arabian	al-Kashi (1427 AD)	correct to 16 decimal places
European	Ludolph van Ceulen (Germany, 1610)	correct to 35 places
	William Shanks (England, 1873)	correct to 527 places
Modern	G. V. & D. V. Chudnovsky (USA 1989)	to 1 011 196 691 places

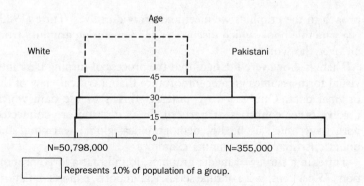

Fig. 3.19. A double bar chart comparing the age structures of the White and Pakistani populations of Great Britain, 1983 (derived from Table 3.5)

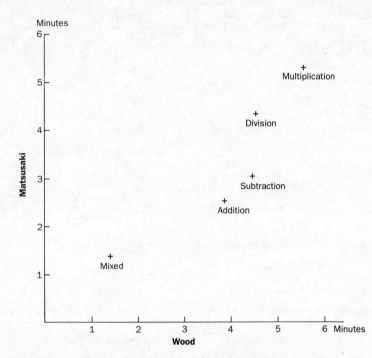

Fig. 3.20. Graph recording the times taken by Kiyoshi Matsusaki (Soroban) and Tom Wood (electric calculator) to complete the batches of computations they attempted in their contest of 1946 (Kojima 1954: 13)

proach to the graphics we meet and draw ourselves. Tufte (1983) is a valuable book which discusses this theme using graphics from all over the world.

There is, however, a danger that the process of turning data into visual form assumes greater importance than a critical view of the original data. One way to counteract this is to use data which involve other countries or parts of the world and are connected with issues such as health, demographics, global warming, and pollution. Chapter 7 contains examples.

Tufte, in a survey of media graphics, found that a large proportion (75 per cent) were of time series, e.g. imports, exports, inflation, and interest rates over time. It is important to include other types of graphic. Fig. 3.20 gives a scatter plot of the celebrated 1946 contest in arithmetic calculation between Matsusaki (Soroban)

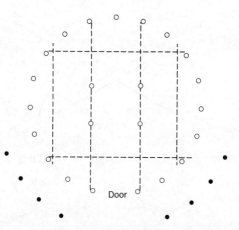

Fig. 3.21. Floor plan of a Kikuyu (Kenyan) cone–cylinder house (Zaslavsky 1973: 160)

of Japan and Private Wood (electric calculator) of the US Armed Forces. It not only provides a good exercise in interpretation of graphics but also invariably arouses interest in the Soroban, the Japanese abacus. Chapter 4 provides information about abacus calculations. See also Kojima (1954).

Spatial concepts

From the beginnings of civilization geometric ideas have been important.

They appear in the design and construction of buildings— domestic and ceremonial—and in civil works such as bridges, fortifications, and embankments.

Zaslavsky (1973) describes the traditional African house, whose cylindrical walls are topped with a conical roof. She gives the floor plan of a Kikuyu (Kenyan) example, showing the post holes (see Fig. 3.21). Some village houses are rectangular; the Kpelle of Liberia lay two poles of equal lengths on the ground, the one across the other, crossing at their midpoints; the ends thus form a rectangle on which the house can be built (see Fig. 3.22).

Many societies had 'rope stretchers' (early Greek: *harpedonapta*; Arabic: *massah*) who were expert in constructing shapes and angles. The construction of a right angle using a loop with twelve

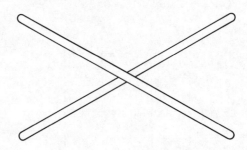

Fig. 3.22. Construction of a rectangle by the Kpelle of Liberia

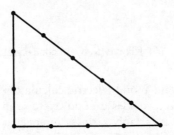

Fig. 3.23. Construction of a right angle using a loop with twelve equally spaced knots

equally spaced knots in it is well known (see Fig. 3.23). But it is less well known that a loop with thirteen knots can be used to obtain an angle close to $\frac{1}{7}$ of 360°, thus providing the basis for an almost perfect construction of a regular heptagon (7-sided polygon) (see Fig. 3.24). This raises the question: what other regular polygons can we construct in this way? For example, can a pentagon be obtained?

The ornamentation of pottery, baskets, and textiles, past and present, shows a world-wide delight in geometrical relationships. Fig 3.25 shows a plaited loop forming a 'starpolygon' with seven vertices, a design which decorates a twelfth-century Persian bowl in the Burrell Collection, Glasgow. As we follow the loop from vertex to vertex we miss out two vertices each time. Apart from enjoying and studying the figure as it stands, are we not tempted to explore the possibility of forming other loops by changing the number of vertices we miss out as we go round, or seeing what

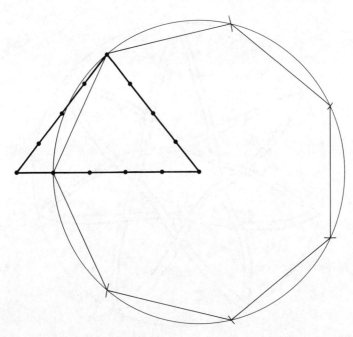

Fig. 3.24. Almost exact construction of a regular heptagon using a loop with thirteen equally spaced knots

other designs can be made if we start with a different number of vertices?

The geometric ideas of congruence and symmetry occur in the 'frieze' or 'strip patterns' which feature in the art of every society. There are seven essentially different types of frieze pattern. Stevens (1981), in his book *Handbook of Regular Patterns*, emphasizes the global appeal of these patterns by exhibiting many examples of each type from different cultures (see Fig. 3.26).

The patterns are distinguished by their symmetries—the geometric transformations which, as it were, copy the pattern on to itself. In the case of the first type, only translations along the strip will do this. In the second case, in addition to translation a further symmetry is a combination of a translation and a reflection in a horizontal line (called a 'glide reflection'). Examples of the different types can be collected in various ways: as an exercise in geometry; by fieldwork; by looking in books of, for example,

Fig. 3.25. Decoration on a twelfth-century Persian bowl (Burrell Collection, Glasgow)

African art. This topic is also discussed in Chapter 6. See also Gallian (1990).

Ratio and proportion

The old arithmetics (and indeed Al-Khwarizmi's *Algebra*) had sections dealing with division of estates. A famous Roman example is:

A dying man wills that, if his wife, being with child, gives birth to a son, the son shall receive $\frac{2}{3}$ and she $\frac{1}{3}$ of his estates: but if a daughter is born, she shall receive $\frac{1}{3}$ and his wife $\frac{2}{3}$. It happens that twins are born, a boy and a girl. How shall the estates be divided so as to satisfy the will?

Young's *Practical Arithmetic* (1864: 116) has the following:

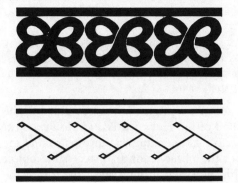

Borneo
L L L L L L

Navaho Indian
L Γ L Γ L Γ

Cretan
V V V'V V V

Sandwich Islands
E E E E E E

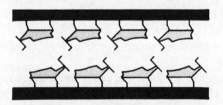

Eskimo
N N N N N N

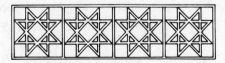

Ghanaian
V Λ V Λ V Λ

Chinese
H H H H H H

Fig. 3.26. Examples of the seven different types of frieze or strip pattern (adapted from Stevens 1981)

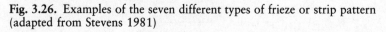

Five persons agree to run a coach between Manchester and York; they provide horses as follows: A 13 miles, B 15 miles, C 12 miles, D 11 miles, and E 9 miles; the proceeds for one month, after paying expenses, amount to £156. Required each person's share.

An impressive use of geometric proportion is contained in the 'double-differences' method of Liu Hui's *Sea Island Mathematical Manual* (c. third century AD). Its main application was to find the height and distance from the observer of an inaccessible object (see Fig. 3.27). First, with the eye at ground level, the top of the object is aligned with the top of the pole. Then the process is repeated with a second pole as shown, the two poles being the same height and in line with the object (see Fig. 3.28). If the poles have height h, are a distance d apart, and the eye is x_1 and x_2 from the base of the pole, then the height H and distance D of the object from the first pole are easily shown, using similar figures, to be given by

$$H = \frac{dh}{x_2 - x_1} + h$$

and

$$D = \frac{dx_1}{x_2 - x_1}$$

Thus knowing h and the two 'differences' d and $x_2 - x_1$ is sufficient to compute H.

Li Yan and Du Shiran (1988) attribute the remarkable accuracy of early Chinese maps to this method of mathematical surveying. It lends itself to school use, and the sensitivity of the method to the accuracy with which x_1 and x_2 are measured is instructive.

Tufte (1983) gives two delightful examples from different continents of graphics which are out of proportion. In Fig. 3.29 the improvement in miles per gallon from 1978 to 1985 is from 18 to $27\frac{1}{2}$ and thus 53 per cent. But the increase in the width of the road is from 0.6 inches to 5.3 inches, which is 783 per cent and fifteen times the actual percentage increase. Tufte gives this graphic a lie factor* of 15. In this case the lines on the road do not fairly represent fuel consumption. Failure to represent magnitudes by

---

* Lie factor = $\dfrac{\text{size of effect shown in graphic}}{\text{size of effect in data}}$.

Fig. 3.27. Measuring the height of an island crag by the 'double-differences' method (Needham 1959: 572)

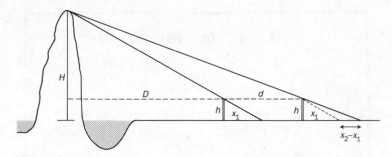

Fig. 3.28. The 'double-differences' survey method

This line, representing 18 miles per
gallon in 1978, is 0.6 inches long.

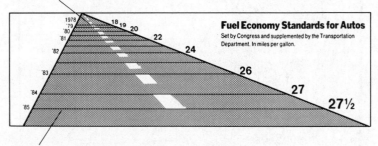

This line, representing 27.5 miles per
gallon in 1985, is 5.3 inches long.

Fig. 3.29. A misleading graphic (Tufte 1983: 57)

correct areas is much more common. Tufte attributes Fig. 3.30
to the 'Pravda School of Ordinal Graphics'. The trend is crystal
clear but the radii of the circles should be in the ratio of $1 : 5 : 17 : 22\frac{1}{2} : 23$.

Statistical ideas

Statistics is an ideal medium for a global approach. On the one
hand it provides and involves children with information about
their world, while on the other hand it calls on arithmetic, meas-

Fig. 3.30. Another misleading graphic (Tufte 1983: 76)

urement, drawing, and inference. My classroom experiences with Zipf's Law are illustrative. The Law states that, if the populations of the towns in a country are ranked and the logarithm of the population of a town is plotted against the logarithm of its rank, then the points lie close to a straight line.* Fig. 3.31 shows the plot for China (1970). Intrigued by this the class tried to find an approximate relation between rank R and population P. But this in turn led to an investigation of other countries—Brazil, Belgium, etc.—and a comparison of results.

Besides descriptive statistics and inference, the other fundamental idea is that of probability. It is fair to say that this subject was born when Fermat (1601–65) and Pascal (1623–62) corresponded over the 'problem of points' (e.g. 'In a game of equal chance A needs 3 and B needs 2 points to win. The game is interrupted and abandoned. How should A and B divide the stake money?') And the topic of games of chance is well worth exploring for material.

An obvious source is games involving dice and a board. Our school textbooks rarely venture far from games involving one or two dice. In, for example, Snakes and Ladders one die is rolled. The scores 1, 2, 3, 4, 5, 6 are assumed to be equally likely:

---

* The law also applies to the frequencies of the commonest words in a language.

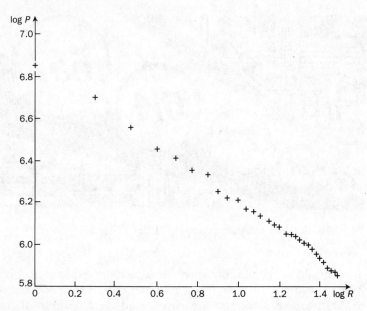

Fig. 3.31. Rank-population data for China (1970) satisfying the approximate relationship $P \simeq 7.2 \times 10^6 \times R^{-0.65}$ (Nelson 1977: 89)

score	1	2	3	4	5	6
probability	$\frac{1}{6}$	$\frac{1}{6}$	$\frac{1}{6}$	$\frac{1}{6}$	$\frac{1}{6}$	$\frac{1}{6}$

In a game such as Monopoly two dice are rolled. The score can be any integer from 2 to 12 and is the sum of the scores of two dice. These scores are not equally likely:

score	2	3	4	5	6	7	8	9	10	11	12
probability	$\frac{1}{36}$	$\frac{2}{36}$	$\frac{3}{36}$	$\frac{4}{36}$	$\frac{5}{36}$	$\frac{6}{36}$	$\frac{5}{36}$	$\frac{4}{36}$	$\frac{3}{36}$	$\frac{2}{36}$	$\frac{1}{36}$

Classroom activities exploring these situations are commonplace. Children roll one or two dice many times and tabulate experimental results. Alternatively the computer can be used. In BASIC a single fair die can be simulated by means of RND(6). This takes the values 1, 2, 3, 4, 5, 6 with equal probability. Similarly RND(6) + RND(6) will simulate tossing two dice and adding their scores.

If we look at games played elsewhere in the world, we find a wide variety of objects and scoring procedures are used. Amongst the objects are pyramidal dice, coins, two-sided dice (one side flat,

Table 3.8. Scoring for some board games in which four 'dice' are thrown

Result of throw (no. of 'heads')	Score			
	Nyout	Zohn Ahl	Pulic	Tablan
0	4	10	5	12
1	1	1	1	2
2	2	2	2	0
3	3	3	3	0
4	5	6	4	8

Source: Ball (1989).

one curved), and cowrie shells. On such dice, one face is marked or designated 'heads', a fixed number are thrown at each turn, and the score is based on the numbers of dice which fall showing 'heads' (or, in the case of cowrie shells, falling with their openings uppermost).

Table 3.8 shows scoring systems for some games using four 'dice'. The games are Nyout from Korea, Zohn Ahl from North America, Pulic from Central America, and Tablan from India (see Ball 1989). Like our games with cubical dice, these games can be explored in the classroom:

- experimentally, by using coins, drawing pins, shells, etc.,
- theoretically (what, for example, if coins are used, is the average score in each of these games?),
- by computer simulation.

When working theoretically or with a computer, assumptions will have to be made about the probability (P) of a single 'die' falling with the marked face or 'head' uppermost. The theoretical approach almost requires the binomial theorem, but the computer simulation is easily achieved. A loop such as

```
HEADS = 0
FOR I = 1 TO 4
HEADS = HEADS + INT(RND(1) + P)
NEXT I
```

will count the number of heads showing after a throw and it is straightforward to write a program which allows you to input the

Table 3.9. Results of a computer simulation of 100 throws of the 'dice' in the game of Nyout

Result of throw (no. of 'heads')	Score	Frequency
0	4	3
1	1	25
2	2	37
3	3	28
4	5	7
Number of throws	100	
Value of P	0.5	
Average score	2.3	

scoring system of the game, the probability (P) of a head, and the number of throws required. The results of a simulation of Nyout are shown in Table 3.9. Bell and Cornelius (1988) is a useful source of information.

This completes our work on the ten key topics. It is fitting to conclude with the computer, because a number of topics have been explored in this way by our students and would make good projects for older pupils in schools; the following programs could be developed:

- to convert a number in modern notation to another notation (e.g. Roman, Chinese), and vice versa,
- to teach Vedic multiplication of two- and three-digit numbers,
- to demonstrate the execution of the 'division method' for square roots.

4 Multiplication Algorithms

GEORGE GHEVERGHESE JOSEPH

Introduction

Observe a group of primary-school children, not as yet introduced to any multiplication algorithm, trying to tackle the following problem:

multiply 24 by 8

Many children would state the problem as '24 times 8', which implies the algorithm of repeated addition. Left to themselves, they are likely to use methods involving a combination of counting, addition, or doubling algorithms with which they are already familiar. A few children may even attempt to solve the problem with methods which show an 'intuitive' grasp of place value and the distributive law. Consider just a few of the algorithms which the children may devise themselves.

A Simple Counting Algorithm

The child simply lists a counting sequence from 1 to 192, as shown below, consisting of numbers up to the eighth multiple of 24. Thus,

1, 2 ... 24 | 25, 26 ... 48 | 49, 50 ... 72 |
73, 74 ... 96 | ... | 169, 170 ... 192 |

A Mixed Counting and Doubling Algorithm

Here the counting sequence continues until 96, when that number is then doubled to get the answer 192.

A Repeated Addition Algorithm

$24 \times 8 = 24 + 24 + 24 + \ldots + 24 = 192$

A Mixed Addition and Doubling Algorithm

$$24 \times 8 = 2(24) + 2(24) + 2(24) + 2(24) = 48 + 48 + 48 + 48$$
$$= 192$$
or
$$24 \times 8 = 2(24) + 2(24) + 2(24) + 2(24) = 2(48) + 2(48)$$
$$= 96 + 96 = 192$$

Other Algorithms

$$24 \times 8 = (20 \times 8) + (4 \times 8) = 192$$
$$24 \times 8 = \{(20 \times 5) + (4 \times 5)\} + \{(20 \times 3) + (4 \times 3)\} = 192$$

Clearly, the 'other algorithms' appear only exceptionally, for they indicate a highly developed 'number' sense. A child who devises algorithms of this kind should have no problem coping with place value in conventional multiplication. But for the vast majority of children, while they are unlikely to have serious problems understanding multiplication structures, there is a difficult conceptual jump between counting, the basis of the adding or doubling algorithm, and the use of place value. This may not appear a serious problem for most adults, for they have already taken on board the point that the numbers used for counting are part of an ordered place-value system. There is, therefore, no logical difficulty in understanding that a three-digit meter in a tape recorder or a car would show the reading 000 after 999. However, a small child taught addition and subtraction through counting may develop a psychological block. The process of counting involves associating names with numbers without due consideration of the place-value principle implied in our base-10 number structure. Or, in the minds of many children, 'ten', 'eleven', and 'twelve' are numbers which follow after 'nine'. They are not the start of a new cycle of numbers. Even the fact that they are written down as 10, 11, and 12 is of little significance, since they are merely arbitrary symbols to represent the three numbers that follow 9, as arbitrary as associating particular spellings with particular words. Unless the concept of place value is already understood, the use of counting as an addition algorithm could inhibit the development of understanding of standard multiplication skills among young children.*

Many primary schools are aware of the difficulty that children have with place value. They often tackle this by an imaginative use of Cuisenaire rods or the Dienes multibase blocks in their preparatory work. But there are other ways of highlighting the nature and versatility of our numeral system for undertaking arithmetic operations, and especially multiplication. For new ideas, we call upon both historical and cultural illustrations of an activity of such universal interest.

It is useful here to distinguish between two modes of performing multiplication that were popular in the past. The first arose in cultures which, either because of scarcity of writing materials or because of the limitations of their numeral systems, resorted to physical devices such as counting rods or an abacus to carry out multiplications. We shall examine one such device that is still in popular use in the market-places and homes of Asia and Africa, namely the abacus, with its diverse variants. The second mode involves 'paper-and-pencil' methods for written numbers. Here, the specific multiplication algorithm chosen in each case depends partly on the nature of the numeral system and partly on the technical expertise of the user. We begin by examining the multiplication algorithm with Egyptian numerals, since this procedure has some similarity to certain methods used by children in multiplication which we discussed earlier. We continue with a discussion of four other procedures—Gelosia multiplication, its variant using Napier's Bones, and two Vedic methods, the *Urdhva Tiryak* and *Nikhilam sutras*. Tailor-made for a place-value numeral system such as ours, these techniques were important in the past and are of relevance for schools today.

---

* The other hurdle that a child has to overcome before being able to do long multiplication is to know the multiplication tables. With the spread of the calculator, this is increasingly viewed as an onerous and irrelevant task. At the same time there is a growing awareness of the dangers of overdependence on calculators. Appendix I shows how multiplication tables can be both mathematically 'productive' and 'palatable'.

A device for multiplication: the Chinese abacus

Early societies possessed neither a suitable numeral system nor accessible writing material for purposes of arithmetical calculations. They had, therefore, to depend on methods which involved different computational devices. A generic term, the *abacus*, was often used in the past to describe any computational device. For the sake of clarity, we will maintain the rather artificial distinction between the words 'computation', where a physical or mechanical device is involved, and 'calculation', which requires working to be written down.

The Latin word, *abacus*, is derived from the Greek word *abax*, which in turn has a Semitic origin in the word *abaq*, meaning a 'drawing board covered in dust'. In its earliest form, the abacus consisted of a wooden surface covered with sand or fine dust on which marks were made and erased easily. It is interesting in this context that, as late as the tenth century, when the Indian numerals found their way to Spain, they were referred to as the Gobar (or dust) numerals, meaning that they were written on a dust abacus.

It was only a matter of time before the dust abacus was replaced by another device, which consisted of a ruled surface, made of wood or stone, of parallel columns representing various powers of ten, on which counters made of glass, bone, or stone were placed in appropriate columns to indicate numbers. The Romans referred to these counters as *calculi*, from which derives the word 'calculate'.

This type of abacus was used in Europe as late as the seventeenth century. However, in certain parts of the world, as early as the beginning of the Christian era, there arose a third type of abacus, where, instead of lines on which counters were placed, a frame was constructed with grooves or rods on which balls or discs could move freely. This would appear to be the ancestor of the modern abacus, in which pierced beads moving up or down on wooden or metal rods are permanently attached to the frame. With the spread of Indian numerals for arithmetical calculations, the abacus has become a toy, with restricted use in classrooms for early work on numbers. As a computational device it now survives mainly in the Far East, notably in China and Japan.

It seems unlikely that the abacus was an indigenous product of the Far East. There is no mention of it in any historical records of

China before the eleventh century AD. The most common device for computation both in China and Japan was counting rods. The abacus was probably brought into China from the Islamic world in the West around the tenth century AD. The fact that the Chinese took it and used it extensively is probably a reflection of the nature of their number system. The Chinese did not adopt the Indian numeral system for calculations until much later. Their rod numerals served as efficient devices for computation until the emergence of the abacus.

The scope of the Chinese abacus as a computational device was significantly increased by a design innovation. Unlike its Western counterpart, which has nine beads along each column, the Chinese abacus (Fig. 4.1*a*) is divided into two sections by a bar, so that along each column there are two beads above the bar (upper beads) and five below the bar (lower beads). (The modern Japanese abacus, or *soroban*, has one bead above the bar and four below.) The upper beads are each worth 'five' and the lower beads are each worth one. Starting from right to left, the nine columns can represent units, tens, hundreds, thousands, etc. To represent a number, beads are moved up or down *towards* the bar.

Fig. 4.1*b* shows how the number 5857 is represented on the abacus. On the extreme right column, which represents units, there are two lower beads against the bar and three lower beads away from the bar. There is one upper bead against the bar and one away from the bar. Since each bead above the bar is worth five and each below the bar is worth one, the number shown on the units column is $5 + 2 = 7$. The next column is the tens column. There is only one upper bead against the bar, which means that the number shown on this column is $5 \times 10 = 50$. In a similar fashion, the hundreds and thousands columns are read as 8×100 and 5×1000 respectively. So the whole configuration of beads in Fig. 4.1*b* represents:

$$5000 + 800 + 50 + 7 = 5857$$

To ensure dexterity and speed in operating the abacus, the use of the correct fingers is emphasized, as in typing. We are advised to use the thumb to move the lower beads to the bar, to use the index finger to move the lower beads away from the bar and the middle finger to move the upper beads to and away from the bar.

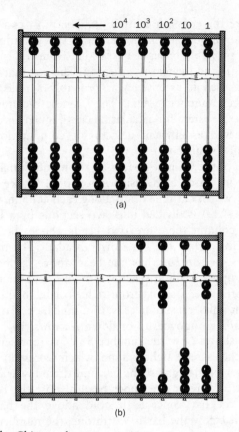

Fig. 4.1a. The Chinese abacus

b. Representation of 5857

It is also important to keep the other fingers curled so that they do not get in the way.

It is in the speed of addition and subtraction that the abacus holds its own against the electronic calculator. Maxwell (1979: 1–2), who provides an invaluable guide to the use of a Chinese abacus, has a test problem consisting of, first, adding a column of eleven numbers and then subtracting four numbers from the result. There is no number of less than three digits and most contain four or five digits. A third-grade abacus operator in China or Japan, possessing the minimum level of competence acceptable for employment in a bank or similar institution, could perform this computation in thirty seconds. Maxwell took ninety seconds working with his calculator. A first-grade operator would have been expected to have finished the computation in twenty seconds. There is even the well-attested claim of an expert operator taking less than fifteen seconds to add ten numbers each of ten digits!

To be able to add with an abacus is not only useful in itself but an essential prerequisite for other arithmetical operations. Figs. 4.2a–c illustrate how this is done in a simple case: 13 + 25. First, the number 13 is recorded on the abacus, as shown in Fig. 4.2a. To add 25, the number is entered by moving two lower beads to the bar in the tens column (see Fig. 4.2b) and one upper bead to the bar in the units column (see Fig. 4.2c). The sum, 38, is shown in Fig. 4.2c.

In more complex additions, attention must be paid both to place value and structural considerations. To illustrate some of the complexities, consider the following problem: 7654 + 9183. Fig. 4.3a shows 7654 entered on an abacus. The addition is performed in the following way:

1. Add 9 thousands to the fourth column in Fig. 4.3a.
   Result: one lower bead against the bar in the fifth column (i.e. the ten thousands column) and one upper and lower bead against the bar in the fourth column (see Fig. 4.3b).
2. Add 1 hundred to the third column in Fig. 4.3b.
   Result: one upper bead and two lower beads against the bar in the third column (see Fig. 4.3c).
3. Add 8 tens to the second column in Fig. 4.3c.
   Result: one more lower bead against the bar in the third column and three lower beads against the bar in the second column (see Fig. 4.3d).
4. Add 3 units to the first column in Fig. 4.3d.
   Result: one upper bead and two lower beads against the bar in the first column (see Fig. 4.3e).

Fig. 4.3e shows the sum, which is easily read as 16837. Note that with an abacus it does not matter in what order you add the columns.

Multiplication involves a different initial set of configuration of beads. To multiply 436 by 8, first the multiplier (i.e. 8) is entered

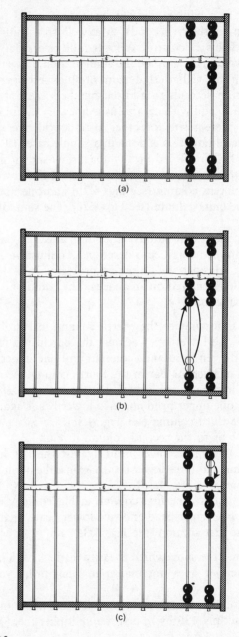

Fig. 4.2a. 13

   b. 13 + 20

   c. 33 + 5 = 38

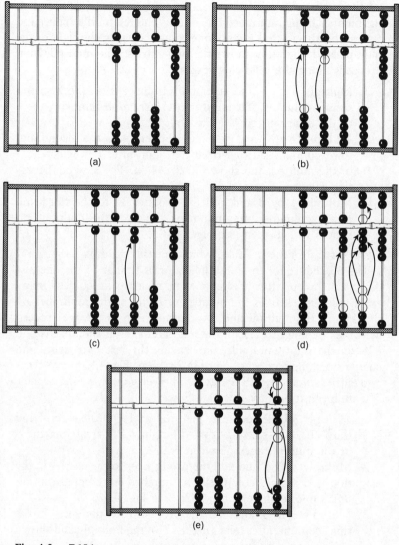

Fig. 4.3a. 7654

   b. 7654 + 9000

   c. 16654 + 100

   d. 16754 + 80

   e. 16834 + 3 = 16837

on the left-hand side of the abacus and then the multiplicand or the number being multiplied (i.e. 436) is entered on the right-hand side of the abacus, but leaving one column clear to the right of the multiplicand. Fig. 4.4a shows the two entries. The multiplication proceeds along the following stages:

1. Multiply 6 by 8 and enter the product 48 on the first and second columns, starting from the right *after* removing the 6 of the multiplicand (see Fig. 4.4b).
2. Multiply 3 by 8 and add the product 24 to the second and third columns starting from the right, after removing the 3 of the multiplicand shown in Fig. 4.4a. The new configuration is given in Fig. 4.4c.
3. Multiply 4 by 8 and add the product 32 to the third and fourth columns, after removing the 4 of the multiplicand shown in Fig. 4.4a (see Fig. 4.4d).

Fig. 4.4d shows the product, which is easily read as 3488.

The procedure for long multiplication is similar to the one just discussed, except that it is important to leave initially as many extra columns clear as the number of digits of the multiplier on the right of the multiplicand. To multiply 638 by 28, we proceed as earlier by entering 28 on the left-hand side of the abacus and 638 on the right-hand side, but leaving the last two right-hand columns (i.e. the number of digits in 28) clear. Fig. 4.5a shows these two entries. Note that 28 is entered in reverse order on the abacus. The multiplication proceeds as follows:

1. Multiply 8 by 2 and enter the product 16 on the second and third columns starting from the right, after removing the 8 of the multiplicand shown in Fig. 4.5a.
2. Multiply 8 by 8 and add the product 64 to the entries in the first and second columns. The number represented on columns one to three is now 224 (see Fig. 4.5b).
3. Multiply 3 by 2 and add the product 6 to the entry in the third column, after removing the 3 of the multiplicand shown in Fig. 4.5a. The number represented on columns one to three is now 824.
4. Multiply 3 by 8 and add the product 24 to the entry in the second and third columns. The number represented on columns one to four is now 1064 (see Fig. 4.5c).

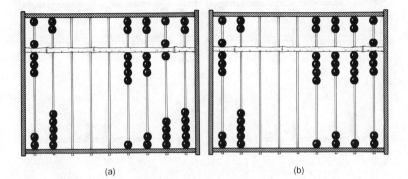

(a)   (b)

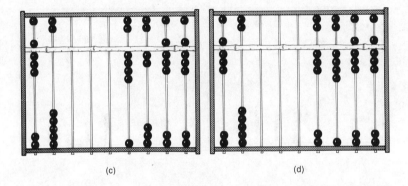

(c)   (d)

Fig. 4.4a. 8 × 436

    b. Multiply 6 by 8 and show 48 on the first and second columns (after removing the 6 of the multiplicand)

    c. Multiply 3 by 8 and add 24 on the second and third columns (after removing the 3 of the multiplicand)

    d. Multiply 4 by 8 and add 32 on the third and fourth columns (after removing the 4 of the multiplicand). The answer: 3488

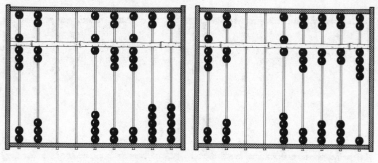

(a)   (b)

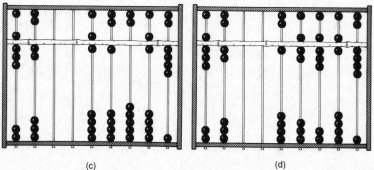

(c)   (d)

Fig. 4.5a. 28 × 638

    b.

    c.

    d. 28 × 638 = 17 864

5. Multiply 6 by 2 and add the product 12 to the entry in the fourth and fifth columns, after removing the 6 of the multiplicand shown in Fig. 4.5*a*. The number represented on columns one to five is 13 064.
6. Multiply 6 by 8 and add the product 48 to the entries in the third and fourth columns.

The number represented on columns one to five in Fig. 4.5*d* is 17864, which is the answer.

The following multiplication algorithm is implied:

$$
\begin{aligned}
638 \times 28 &= (8 + 20) \times 638 \\
&= (8 \times 8) + (20 \times 8) + (8 \times 30) + (20 \times 30) \\
&\quad + (8 \times 600) + (20 \times 600) \\
&= 17\,864
\end{aligned}
$$

This odd way of carrying out multiplication may have something to do with the fact that the abacus has no 'memory'!

The abacus that one buys in toy shops would be of only limited value for such computations. It is the bar dividing the abacus into two parts, one for fives and the other for units, that extends the scope and versatility of the Chinese abacus. In the early stages of work in arithmetic the Chinese abacus is particularly suitable, since it provides a natural extension to counting in fives on fingers. Moreover, it serves to enhance a child's understanding of concepts such as 'carrying', 'borrowing', and 'place value', provided in a concrete mode and therefore more easy to comprehend than from books or the blackboard. In any case, to 'learn by playing' is a valuable option for young children, whose concentration span is limited and for whom the relevance of what they are learning is not immediately obvious. But, having said that, it should be recognized that the electronic calculator is overwhelmingly superior to an abacus in that the latter first has no memory, secondly requires a long training period to achieve proficiency, and thirdly is less convenient to carry around.

Egyptian multiplication

The Egyptians developed one of the earliest methods of written multiplication over four thousand years ago. As explained in

Chapter 3 (pp. 48–50), they worked with a set of hieroglyphic numerals representing each successive power of 10 from 10^0 or 1 up to 10^6 or a million (see Fig. 3.4). Any number can be written using these symbols additively.

So

$$12\,013 = 3 + 1(10) + 2(10^3) + 1(10^4) = \;|||\; \cap \; \underset{\Delta}{\int^{\mathfrak{d}}} \; \underset{\Delta}{\int^{\mathfrak{d}}} \; \mathfrak{g}$$

No difficulties arise from *not* having a symbol for zero in this numeral system. It is also a matter of little consequence in what order the hieroglyphs appear, though the practice was generally to list them from right to left in a descending order of magnitude, as shown in the example above. Additions and subtractions pose few problems. In adding two numbers, one makes a collection of each set of symbols that appears in both numbers and then replaces them with the next higher symbol when necessary. Subtraction involves merely a reversal of the process of addition, with 'borrowing' achieved by replacing a larger hieroglyph by ten of the next lower-order symbol.

The great merit of the Egyptian method of multiplication is that it requires knowledge of only addition and the 'two-times' table. All the tedium and effort going into the learning of multiplication tables is thus avoided. To illustrate, take this example:

multiply 28 by 13

The Egyptian scribe who is carrying out the calculation has to first decide which of the two numbers is the *multiplicand*. Suppose he (for the scribe we know was always a male!) chose 28. He writes down 28 and by continually multiplying by 2 obtains its products with 2, 4, 8 . . . Fig. 4.6 shows how this information is set down.

The doubling process stops at the point where the next entry in the left-hand column would exceed the multiplier 13. Numbers in the left-hand column which add up to 13 are selected (asterisked in Fig. 4.6) and their corresponding products with 28 in the right-hand column are added to give the required result: 364.

For this method to be used in multiplication of any two integers, the following rule must apply:

> every integer can be expressed as the sum of the integral powers of 2

Egyptian notation		Modern notation	
* I IIII / IIII ∩∩		* I	28
II III ∩∩∩ / III ∩∩		2	56
* IIII II ∩ 𝟫		* 4	112
* IIII / IIII IIII ∩∩𝟫𝟫		* 8	224
∩∩∩ / IIII ∩∩∩ 𝟫 𝟫 𝟫	1+4+8=13	28+112+224=$\underline{\underline{364}}$	

Fig. 4.6. Multiplying the Egyptian way: 28 × 13

Thus

$$15 = 2^0 + 2^1 + 2^2 + 2^3$$
$$23 = 2^0 + 2^1 + 2^2 + 2^4$$

It is not known whether the Egyptians were aware of the general applicability of this rule, though the confidence with which they approached all forms of multiplication by this process of 'duplation' would incline one to believe that they were. This rule is applied today in the design of high-speed electronic computers.

This ancient method of multiplication provides the foundation for the entire art of Egyptian calculation. It was widely used, with some variations, by the Greeks and continued well into the Middle Ages in Europe. A variation on this method, still popular in rural communities of Russia, Ethiopia, the Arab world, and the Near East, is known in the West as the Russian Peasant method. Again, the method can be illustrated by an example:

multiply 225 by 17

The method involves continually doubling one of the numbers (17) and halving the other (225) but leaving out any remainder. The process continues until the number that is being halved becomes 1. See Fig. 4.7, where the number which is being halved is in the left-hand column, and the number which is doubled is in the right-hand column. Any row with an even number in the left-hand column is then crossed out, and the remaining numbers in the right-hand column are added together to get the answer. The

225	17
~~112~~	~~34~~
~~56~~	~~68~~
~~28~~	~~136~~
~~14~~	~~272~~
7	544
3	1088
1	2176
	3825

Fig. 4.7. The Russian Peasant method: 225×17

method works because 225 can be expressed as the sum of the integral powers of 2, i.e.

$$225 = 1(2^7) + 1(2^6) + 1(2^5) + 0(2^4) + 0(2^3) + 0(2^2) + 0(2^1) + 1(2^0)$$

The sum of the products of these components with 17 (i.e. the product of the binary number 11100001 with 17) gives the answer 3825.

Gelosia or Lattice Multiplication

In 1494 the Italian Luca Pacioli (c.1445–1517) published his *Summa*, which contains a description of eight different methods of carrying out multiplication, including methods in common use today. Though none of the methods discussed in the text is original, since earlier versions are found—notably in the works of Indian mathematicians, Mahavira (c. AD 850) and Bhaskaracharya (c. AD 1150)—Pacioli's systematic treatment of the various multiplication algorithms provides a useful starting-point for our discussion. Of these methods, we examine one, Gelosia multiplication, which is no longer popular, though it was widely used in Europe

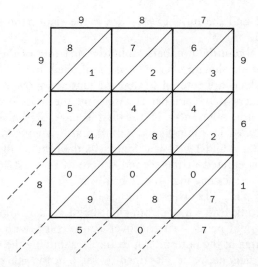

Fig. 4.8. Gelosia multiplication: 987 × 961

before the appearance of printed mathematics texts. After discussing a procedure derived from this and named after the inventor of logarithms, John Napier, we describe two methods which are usually referred to as Vedic, of which the first was known to Pacioli.

Gelosia or lattice multiplication owes its name to the arrangement of multiplication to resemble a medieval grating or lattice, which custom dictated should be placed at windows of houses to shield women from public gaze. The method makes its first appearance in India around the tenth century, from where it spread into Arab mathematics. It proved highly popular and soon found its way to Italy, probably through Sicily, which was an important centre of Arab learning. It appears in a number of European manuscripts between the fourteenth and fifteenth centuries. To illustrate the procedure, take an example from Pacioli's text:

multiply 987 by 961

The solution proceeds in the following stages:

1. Construct a three-by-three grid, as shown in Fig. 4.8. Draw the diagonals and enter the number 987 across the top of the

      grid and the number 961 down the right-hand side of the grid.

2. To obtain the numbers along the first row of the grid, each digit of the number 987 is multiplied by 9. The partial products are entered so that the tens are above the diagonal in each of the smaller squares and the units below it. For example, the entry in the first square of the first row is obtained by multiplying 9 by 9 and 8 is entered above the diagonal and 1 below it. Similarly, the product of 8 and 9 or 72 is entered in the second square of the first row, with 7 above the diagonal and 2 below it.

3. Complete all entries in the grid.

4. Starting from the bottom right-hand corner, add along the diagonal paths, carrying over if necessary, with the results written at the bottom. For example, summing the numbers in the diagonal path (identified by the 6 at the side of the grid) gives 2 + 0 + 8 = 10, so 0 is written at the bottom and 1 carried over to the summing of the next diagonal path (identified by the 9 at the side of the grid), which gives 3 + 4 + 8 + 0 + 9 = 24 *plus* 'carry' 1 to give 25. In the same way, the sum of the diagonal path identified by the 7 at the top of the grid is 6 + 2 + 4 + 4 + 0 = 16 plus 'carry' 2 to give 18. Repeating this procedure for all diagonal paths and reading the diagonal sums down starting from the top left-hand side and then right along the bottom row gives the answer 948 507.

This method is interesting for a number of reasons. From the point of view of a child who comes across the method for the first time, knowledge of multiplication tables to 9 and the ability to add are all that is required. The hurdles of 'carrying' and of place value are postponed until the final stage, when addition along the diagonal paths takes place. A child who finds it difficult to cope with all the complications posed by the usual multiplication algorithms may benefit from being introduced to this method, especially since the familiar multiplication algorithm may have evolved from the older method. To illustrate with the example just discussed, the multiplication algorithm which we know is shown in Fig. 4.9. The final answer is obtained in the same way as the

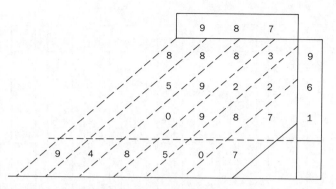

Fig. 4.9. A modified Gelosia multiplication: 987×961

Gelosia method by adding along the diagonal, with the difference that, in the present method, partial products are recorded *after* adding the 'carries' at each stage of calculation. The elimination of the lattice lines, the rearrangement of the multiplier (961) beneath the multiplicand (987), and starting multiplication with the units digit of the multiplier (i.e. 1) instead of the highest-place digit (i.e. 9) produces the familiar multiplication algorithm. It is quite likely that the Gelosia method may have still been popular, were it not for some of the technical problems of printing the lattice lines as well as the numbers in the grid.

Napier's Bones

The Gelosia method is also interesting for another reason. It may be seen as the basis of an important invention known as Napier's rods (or bones). In 1617 the Scotsman, John Napier (1550–1617), was responsible for the next important development in mechanical computational device after the abacus. A man of considerable ingenuity, imagination, and strong prejudices, he was seen by some as a master of witchcraft. His fame today rests on his invention of logarithms. He also constructed a series of rods which came to be known as Napier's bones.

Fig. 4.10*a* shows a simplified version of these rods. They are numbered in the top row from 1 to 9 and, in the eight divisions below, each of these numbers is multiplied by 2, 3, 4 . . . 9 (as indicated by the Index), with the products entered in a similar

(a) Index

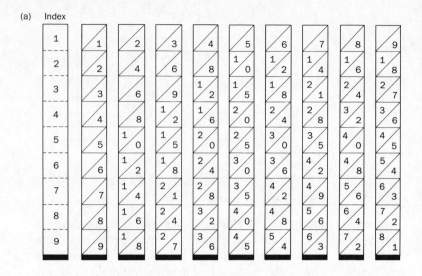

(b) Index

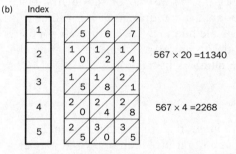

$567 \times 20 = 11340$

$567 \times 4 = 2268$

$567 \times 24 = (567 \times 20) + (567 \times 4) = 11340 + 2268 = 13608$

Fig. 4.10a. Napier's bones

    b. Napier's bones: 567×24

fashion to that used in the Gelosia multiplication grid. These rods (or bones) were mainly used for multiplication and division, as in the following example:

multiply 567 by 24

Fig. 4.10*b* shows the method. Rods headed by 5, 6, and 7 are selected and placed side by side in that order. A section of these rods

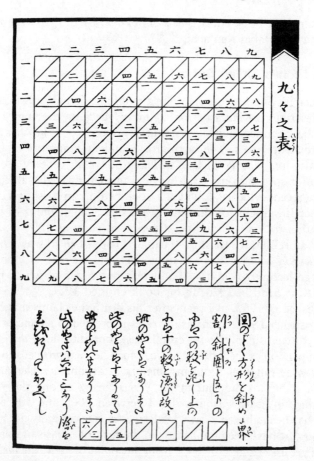

Fig. 4.11. Napier's bones in Japan (from Hanai Kenkichi's *Seisan Sokuchi* (1856), in Smith and Mikami (1914: 262)

is shown in the diagram. The results of 567 × 20 and 567 × 4 are obtained by adding diagonally, as in the Gelosia multiplication, the numbers shown in the shaded squares. The sum of 11 340 and 228 gives the answer.

Napier's bones became very popular in Europe during the seventeenth century, with a number of changes in design to make them more compact and efficient. They were introduced into China at the beginning of the eighteenth century and found their way into Japan a hundred years later. The diagram shown in Fig. 4.11

appears in a book entitled *Seisan Sokuchi* by the Japanese mathematician, Hanai Kenkichi.

The Urdhva Tiryak Sutra

In Pacioli's *Summa* there appears a multiplication algorithm, which he describes as 'fantastic' or 'lightning' because the final answer can be obtained quickly without any need to write down any intermediate steps. The method is found in a number of Indian manuscripts, dating back to at least the eighth century AD, from where it spread to the Arab world and then to medieval Europe. More recent evidence, found in a book by Bharati Krishna Tirthaji, pushes the origins of this and other short-cut methods of multiplication to Vedic India (i.e. a period as early as 1000 BC).

Swami Bharati Krishna Tirthaji (1884–1960) was born in Tinnevely, a town near Madras. In 1911 he left his job as a college lecturer to join a Hindu religious order of which he became the head in 1925. In his book entitled *Vedic Mathematics*, published in 1965, five years after his death, he claims that he has reconstructed sixteen sutras (or rules expressed in a concise form) and thirteen sub-sutras (or corollaries) contained in a *Parisista* (or an appendix) of the *Atharva Veda*, which he then proceeds to apply to a wide range of problems, mainly in arithmetic. The *Atharva Veda* is one of the four major Vedas, being among the earliest writings in India variously dated between 1000 and 500 BC. No one has been able to locate this *Parisista*. It is certainly not among those that have been published. So the historical basis of this book is as yet uncertain. However, from our point of view, the historical authenticity of the book is less important than the insights that it provides into the scope and strength of our numeral system, particularly when it comes to multiplication.

In this chapter we consider two of the sutras which apply to long multiplication, starting with the one that made such a deep impression on Pacioli: the Urdhva Tiryak sutra. A translation of this sutra from Sanskrit reads:

vertically and crosswise

As it stands, the instruction is cryptic to the point of incomprehension. This type of conciseness is a characteristic found in many of the mathematical texts of ancient and medieval India, which enabled the contents to be easily memorized. Bharati Tirthaji may have performed a similar function to many Indian commentators before him, to elaborate and illustrate cryptic sutras with well-chosen examples. Let us take a few examples of multiplication where the sutra applies:

multiply 36 by 53

The solution is set out as follows:

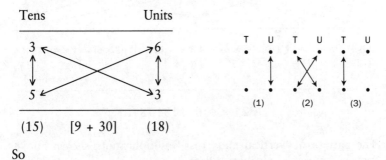

(15)   [9 + 30]   (18)

So

$$36 \times 53 = 1908$$

The method is indicated by the words of the sutra, 'vertically and crosswise'. First, the numbers in the units column are multiplied vertically (i.e. $6 \times 3 = 18$). Next the units and tens digits are multiplied crosswise and added (i.e. $(3)(3) + (6)(5) = 39$). Then the numbers in the tens column are multiplied vertically (i.e. $3 \times 5 = 15$). Finally, place-value adjustments are made by 'carrying over' the relevant numbers. The whole multiplication process is shown by the diagram where the sequence of operations is labelled (1) to (3).

Why does the method work? The explanation is found if the numbers are expressed in an algebraic form. We know that

$$36 = 3x + 6, \qquad 53 = 5x + 3 \qquad \text{where } x = 10$$

So that multiplying 36 by 53 is equivalent to

$$(3x + 6)(5x + 3) = 15x^2 + 39x + 18$$

Or, more generally,

$$(ax + b)(cx + d) = acx^2 + (ad + bc)x + bd$$

Now consider the following multiplication:

multiply 324 by 416

The solution is set out as follows:

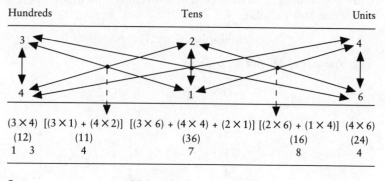

Hundreds		Tens		Units
3	2			4
4	1			6

(3×4)	$[(3 \times 1) + (4 \times 2)]$	$[(3 \times 6) + (4 \times 4) + (2 \times 1)]$	$[(2 \times 6) + (1 \times 4)]$	(4×6)
(12)	(11)	(36)	(16)	(24)
1 3	4	7	8	4

So $\qquad$ $324 \times 416 = 134\,784$

The pattern of 'vertical and cross' multiplication, shown above, may be expressed algebraically, as:

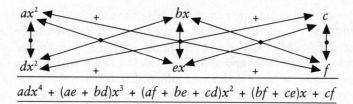

$$adx^4 + (ae + bd)x^3 + (af + be + cd)x^2 + (bf + ce)x + cf$$

where, in the above case, $a = 3$, $b = 2$, $c = 4$, $d = 4$, $e = 1$, and $f = 6$, and $x = 10$

This method can be applied to cases where the two numbers have any number of digits. If the number of digits in one is not equal to the other, then adjustments are made, filling in zeros to the left of the smaller number. It is interesting in this context that both the Arabs and the medieval Europeans did this as a matter of course.

Let us conclude with an illustration showing the multiplication of a three-digit number by a four-digit number.*

multiply 2341 by 683

The solution is set out as follows:

Thousands	Hundreds	Tens	Units
2	3	4	1
0	6	8	3

(2×0) $[12 + 0]$ $[16 + 0 + 18]$ $[6 + 0 + 24 + 24]$ $[9 + 6 + 32]$ $[12 + 8]$ (1×3)

(0)	(12)	(34)	(54)	(47)	(20)	3
1	5	9	8	9	0	3

So $\qquad$ 2341 × 683 = 1 598 903

The pattern of the calculation is summarized below in Fig. 4.12. The large dots represent digits and the lines joining them show the figures to be multiplied. The order of the calculation is indicated by Steps 1–7. This procedure is quite general and can be used to multiply any pair of numbers. However, the difficulty with this method is the level of skill in multiplication and addition assumed and the degree of recall required. The burden on memory can be

---

* This algorithm is best seen in terms of representing any number as the sum of its place digits (a_i where i = 0, 1, 2 . . .) multiplied by the corresponding powers of the modulus of the arithmetic (usually 10 but denoted here by x^i where i = 0, 1, 2, . . .). Let the two numbers to be multiplied be:

$$P = \sum_{i=0}^{\infty} a_i x^i \quad \text{and} \quad Q = \sum_{j=0}^{\infty} b_j x^j$$

Then this algorithm suggests that

$$P \times Q = \sum_{n=0}^{\infty} \left(\sum_{k=0}^{n} a_k b_{n-k} \right) x^n$$

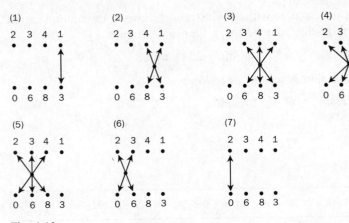

Fig. 4.12

eased to some extent by entering the 'carries' in a separate row. Thus, in solving the given problem, there will be the following two rows, where the second row contains the 'carries':

0	2	4	4	7	0	3
1	3	5	4	2		
1	5	9	8	9	0	3

The method may also prove to be cumbersome and difficult when there are large digits involved. To illustrate:

$$\text{multiply } 589 \text{ by } 678$$

the solution is set out as follows:

	5		8		9
	6		7		8
	0	3	0	7	2
3	8	5	2	7	
	1	1			
3	9	9	3	4	2

The partial products that arise at each stage of computation starting from the right are:

$$(9 \times 8) = 72$$
$$[(8 \times 8) + (9 \times 7)] = 127$$
$$[(5 \times 8) + (6 \times 9) + (8 \times 7)] = 150$$
$$[(5 \times 7) + (6 \times 8)] = 83$$
$$(5 \times 6) = 30$$

The numbers are so large that the 'carries' spill over, requiring even a third row. The mental arithmetic involved in multiplication and addition, even if the 'carries' are written down, can be quite formidable. It is possible to simplify the calculations by making the following transformation, which uses the *vinculum* (or line drawn above certain numbers).

$$589 \equiv 6\,\bar{1}\,\bar{1}$$
$$678 \equiv 7\,\bar{2}\,\bar{2}$$

where $6\,\bar{1}\,\bar{1} = 600 - 10 - 1$ and $7\,\bar{2}\,\bar{2} = 700 - 20 - 2$.
The multiplication is set out as follows:

| | 6 | | $\bar{1}$ | | $\bar{1}$ |
	7		$\bar{2}$		$\bar{2}$
4	2 $\bar{1}$	$\bar{9}$ $\bar{1}$	7	4	2
4	0	0	$\bar{7}$	4	2

Transforming the answer to the more familiar form:

$$4\ 0\ 0\ \bar{7}\ 4\ 2 \equiv 3\ 9\ 9\ 3\ 4\ 2$$

The Nikhilam Sutra

The second of the multiplication sutras, the Nikhilam Sutra, may be translated as:

all from 9 and the last from 10

To explain this rule, let us begin with a simple example. Consider the multiplication of 9 by 8. Both numbers are close to the 'base' number 10. In our numeral system any integral power of ten (such as 10^1, 10^2, 10^3, 10^4, . . .) is a 'base' number. To find the product of 9 and 8, we place the numerals one below the other with their respective complements or 'deficiencies' from 10 (i.e. $10 - 9 = 1$ and $10 - 8 = 2$) to their right. The sutra indicates how these 'deficiencies' are obtained. It is, incidentally, the same transformation rule that we applied to eliminate awkward digits in the previous problem.

$$9 \mid 1$$
$$8 \mid 2$$

The tens digit of the answer is obtained by subtracting diagonally, either 2 from 9 or 1 from 8, each giving 7. The units digit is obtained by multiplying the deficiences (or the two ten-complements) 1 and 2, giving 2.

$$(9 - 2)10 + (2 \times 1) = 72$$

So 72 is the product. The algebraic rationale is easily established. To multiply two numbers a and b, where the numbers are less than ten, find their ten-complements, which are $(10 - a)$ and $(10 - b)$ respectively. The rule states:

$$ab = 10\{a - (10 - b)\} + (10 - a)(10 - b)$$
$$= 10a - 100 + 10b + 100 - 10a - 10b + ab = ab$$

This procedure for multiplication has some real advantages. For one thing there is no need to learn the multiplication tables beyond five. But a more substantial advantage, which probably also explains its ancient origins, is its easy adaptation for finger calculations. To illustrate, take the multiplication of 9 by 8. We begin by representing the ten-complements of 9 and 8 by one standing finger on one hand and two standing fingers on the other respectively. Next multiply the standing fingers for the units digit (i.e. $1 \times 2 = 2$) and add the closed fingers for the tens digit (i.e. $4 + 3 = 7$), giving the answer of 72. This method of multiplication is to be found all over the world, especially in the market-places of Africa and Asia.

This transformation principle can be extended to include all sorts of multiplications. The singular contribution of Indian arithmetic was to devise a series of extensions of this principle, all of which exploit some of the hidden strengths of our place-value numeral system. The method is most effective when at least one of the numbers to be multiplied is near to a power of 10. We will illustrate the scope of the algorithm with the help of a few examples. An algebraic rationale is provided in each case.

multiply 88 by 96

The solution is set out as follows:

Number	Deficiency (100)	Algebraic Explanation
88	12	Let x (or the base) be the power of 10 nearest to the two numbers (or 100 in this case). Let c and d
96	4	be the 'deficiencies' of the two numbers to be multiplied from x.
84	48	

Then

$$(x - c)(x - d) = x(x - c - d) + cd$$

Or applying the formula

So $88 \times 96 = 8448$

$$(100 - 12)(100 - 4)$$
$$= 100(100 - 12 - 4) + 48$$
$$= 8400 + 48 = 8448$$

The power of 10 nearest to the two numbers is $10^2 = 100$, which we will refer to as the base. Subtract 88 and 96 from the base to get the 'deficiencies' 12 and 4 respectively. Express these calculations as given above. The product will consist of two components on either side of the vertical line.

The number 84 is obtained from cross-subtraction:

$$88 - 4 = 84 \text{ or } 96 - 12 = 84$$

The number 48 is obtained by taking the product of the deficiencies, which is:

$$12 \times 4 = 48$$

The final answer is obtained from merging the two parts or 8448.

multiply 1038 by 1006

The solution is set out as follows:

Number (1000)	Surplus	Algebraic Explanation
1038	38	Let x be the base and c and d be the 'surpluses'
1006	6	
1044	228	Then

$$(x + c)(x + d) = x(x + c + d) + cd$$

Or applying the formula

$$(1000 + 38)(1000 + 6)$$
$$= 1000(1000 + 38 + 6) + 228$$
$$= 1\,044\,228$$

So $\qquad\qquad 1038 \times 1006 = 1\,044\,228$

The method is the same as in the previous example, except we deal here in 'surpluses'.

multiply 128 by 89

The solution is set out as follows:

Number	Surplus/ (Deficiency) (100)	Algebraic Explanation
128	28	Let x be the base and c and d be the 'surplus' and 'deficiency' respectively
89	(11)	
117	(308)	Then
117 − 4	100 − 8	$(x + c)(x - d) = x(x + c - d) - cd$
113	92	Or applying the formula

$$(100 + 28)(100 - 11)$$
$$= 100(100 + 28 - 11) - 308$$
$$= 11\,392$$

So   128 × 89 = 11 392

The method is slightly more involved than in the previous examples. The numbers and their 'surplus' or 'deficiency' are arranged in the usual way. The left-hand side is obtained by either cross-subtraction (i.e. 128 − 11 = 117) or cross-addition (i.e. 89 + 28 = 117). On the right-hand side, the product of the surplus and deficiency gives a deficiency of 308, which is split up into 3 hundreds and subtracted from 117 on the left-hand side. The last adjustment involves subtracting the 8 that remains from another hundred 'borrowed' from the left-hand side. Thus the whole adjustment reduces the left-hand side by 4, leaving 113.

multiply 497 by 493

We give two solutions:

Number	Deficiency		Number	Deficiency
(100 × 5)			(1000/2)	
497	(03)		497	(003)
493	(07)		493	(007)
490	21	OR	490	021
× 5			× 1/2	
2450	21		245	021

So   497 × 493 = 245 021

In this example an extension of the sutra involves using a temporary base. The numbers 497 and 493 are both close to 500, which becomes the temporary base. The deficiencies from 500 are obtained in the usual way and the solution proceeds along similar lines as in previous examples. However, since a temporary base rather than an actual base (which is always an integral power of 10) is used, an adjustment needs to be made to the left-hand side of the answer (i.e. 490). The solutions above consider two adjustments where in one case the actual base of 100 involves a scale factor of 5 and in the other with an actual base of 1000 a scale factor of 1/2. An algebraic rationale is easily established by incorporating a scale factor f to take account of the transformation from a temporary to an actual base and following the algebraic development shown in the solution to the first example in this section.

There exists a corollary to the Nikhilam sutra which is useful for squaring numbers near a suitable base. It reads:

Whatever the extent of the deficiency, lessen it still further to that very extent; and set up the square (of that deficiency).

To illustrate the application of this rule, consider the simple case of squaring 8 which is near base 10. The rule states that we first find the deficiency (or ten-complement) of 8 which is 2. Next we subtract from 8 this deficiency to give $8 - 2 = 6$. Finally, we square the deficiency which gives 4 and form the answer $8^2 = 64$.

The application of this rule gives:

(i) $9^2 =$ 8 | 1   Base = 10
(ii) $12^2 =$ 14 | 4   Base = 10 (add the surplus
                                        in this case)
(iii) $95^2 =$ 90 | 25   Base = 100
(iv) $108^2 =$ 116 | 64   Base = 100 (add the surplus
                                        in this case)
(v) $9986^2 =$ 9972 | 0196   Base = 10 000

The algebraic rationale for the method is easily established and is given below for the case where x = base and a = surplus/deficiency:

$$(x \pm a)^2 = x(x \pm 2a) + a^2$$

We have only examined one application of the two sutras discussed, namely the operation of multiplication. The range of other possible applications is quite considerable and illustrations will be found in Bharata Tirthaji's book. For example, the 'vertically and crosswise' sutra could be used in: (1) evaluation of determinants; (2) solution of simultaneous linear equations; (3) derivation of trigonometric functions; (4) solution of cubic and higher order equations; and (5) evaluation of logarithms and exponentials. None of these subjects, however, forms part of the elementary school curriculum.

It should be emphasized that I am not making the absurd claim that these subjects were known in ancient times, but that the approach which goes under the name of 'Vedic' methods provides fresh insights into a number of topics.

At the level of long multiplication, this approach is seen to be useful for a number of reasons. First, it emphasizes the strengths of our place-value system which are not fully exploited by the conventional multiplication algorithms. For many children, multiplication proves to be the first major hurdle that they come across in mathematics. The problems posed by knowing multiplication tables, the complexities of 'carrying', 'borrowing', and place value, and the effort of retaining and recalling numbers, are formidable for an average child, especially if these problems arise at the same time. The use of alternative methods may be a way of retaining a child's interest as well as overcoming difficulties in understanding traditional approaches. A number of methods discussed in this chapter, namely Egyptian multiplication and the Gelosia method, are suitable, not as substitutes for existing procedures but as preliminary work.

The Vedic methods have other merits. They provide a fresh insight into elementary operations with our number system. A number is not merely considered as having an existence in itself. It should be looked at in relation to a convenient base. Thus, in multiplying 97 by 103, we are using the facts that the first number is three less than 100 and the second is three in excess of 100. The operation of multiplication is greatly simplified, as we saw in the examples discussed, if it takes place in relation to the defined surplus and deficiency from the base 100.

These methods also bring out clearly the simple though not widely recognized fact that algebra is but a generalization of arithmetic. We found that, in the methods examined, there is always a clear algebraic rationale. But more important still, the methods highlight a less obvious fact, that any polynomial may be expressed in terms of a positional notation without the base being specified. Once this is accepted, the same algorithmic scheme may be applied equally to arithmetic and algebraic problems. The artificial distinction that has grown up between the two subjects, which is a by-product both of increasing specialization and of the existing hierarchy of mathematical knowledge, will cease to be a significant hurdle for children being introduced to algebra for the first time.

Finally, these methods are conducive to encouraging mental

arithmetic, a subject neglected in present-day study of arithmetic. Nobody would deny that the arithmetic of everyday life is more dependent upon mental than written computation. Research into the processes involved in mental arithmetic shows the importance of having a number of reference points, with a skilled calculator being able to pick out quickly the proper reference points. If, for example, you were asked to work out the product of 105 and 103, one approach would be to choose a suitable reference number close to the answer (i.e. 10 000), with a recognition that the answer is in excess of this reference number. The skill in carrying out the final adjustment is an important requirement to achieve competence at mental arithmetic. The Vedic methods help to provide a whole range of reference points, of which identifying the base and utilizing it for multiplication is not only an example but serves as a coherent rationale for the method used and a check on the accuracy of the result obtained. At present, when an overdependence on calculators for simple computations is widespread, often at the expense of losing the skills of mental arithmetic, approaches like the Vedic methods have considerable educational value but, more important, stimulate that disappearing 'appetite for sums' which is the foundation for a life-long passion for the subject.

Appendix: Multiplication tables can be fun

Does learning multiplication tables have to be a boring, unproductive, and socially remote exercise?

Multiplication tables may be presented in a variety of ways. Fig. 4.13 is a display chart of the tables of just the numbers 1 to 9, so that the product of, say, 5 and 8 can be read either from the entry which is the intersection of the 5th row and the 8th column or from the entry which is the intersection of the 8th row and the 5th column. Fig. 4.14 is known as the Vedic Square. It is derived from Fig. 4.13 by successively replacing those entries which exceed 9 by the sum of their digits until a single digit results. For example, from the 8th row and 7th column in Fig. 4.13 we deduce that $8 \times 7 = 56$. The Vedic transformation involves first obtaining the sum $5 + 6 = 11$ and, since 11 exceeds 9, a further transformation gives $1 + 1 = 2$, which the reader may check is the corresponding entry in Fig. 4.14. The figure is referred to as the Vedic Square because of its apparent origins in the *Vedas*, mentioned earlier as being among some of the oldest Indian texts.

Both Fig. 4.13 and Fig. 4.14 could be a rich source of discovery of numerical and geometrical relationships to enliven mathematics classes. They also serve as useful pointers to a number of topics across the school curriculum. It is clearly impractical, given the limited scope of this appendix, to bring out all the patterns and relationships contained in the figures. Instead, we concentrate on the visual patterns (or the 'shapes') generated by the Vedic Square and highlight some of their mathematical aspects.

One of the unfortunate aspects of the way that mathematics has developed over time is its remoteness from a number of other areas of human knowledge which are also interested in order, sequence, pattern, and colour. Art, music, dance, and poetry are examples of disciplines where such concerns are important. It is interesting that, historically, mathematical representations in a number of non-European cultures owed much to these disciplines. A Chinese mathematician distinguished positive from negative quantities using two colours—red for positive and black for negative. An Indian mathematician was often judged not only by the quality of the mathematics but also by the virtuosity displayed in the composition of the verses in which the results were stated. The Incas of South America used a sophisticated device (the Quipu) for recording

×	1	2	3	4	5	6	7	8	9
1	1	2	3	4	5	6	7	8	9
2	2	4	6	8	10	12	14	16	18
3	3	6	9	12	15	18	21	24	27
4	4	8	12	16	20	24	28	32	36
5	5	10	15	20	25	30	35	40	45
6	6	12	18	24	30	36	42	48	54
7	7	14	21	28	35	42	49	56	63
8	8	16	24	32	40	48	56	64	72
9	9	18	27	36	45	54	63	72	81

Fig. 4.13. Multiplication Tables

numerical information in which different colours represented different categories of information. So what may now look like an old mop made out of different coloured knotted strings is in fact a whole population census recorded for posterity.

To us a numeral (or a written number) serves only as a counting or calculating device. Its nature as a visual element or as a stimulus for recalling anything other than a specific quantity is neglected. A young child who is introduced to a numeral system must find its restrictive context first a source of bewilderment and later a source of anxiety. In the world of play, visual images and patterns predominate; and the interaction between the external and internal world of the child, as part of the educational process, is helped by visual conceptualization. An implied

×	1	2	3	4	5	6	7	8	9
1	1	2	3	4	5	6	7	8	9
2	2	4	6	8	1	3	5	7	9
3	3	6	9	3	6	9	3	6	9
4	4	8	3	7	2	6	1	5	9
5	5	1	6	2	7	3	8	4	9
6	6	3	9	6	3	9	6	3	9
7	7	5	3	1	8	6	4	2	9
8	8	7	6	5	4	3	2	1	9
9	9	9	9	9	9	9	9	9	9

Fig. 4.14. The Vedic Square

premiss in the use of the Vedic Square is that numbers have 'shapes', just as objects.

To find the 'shape' of the number 1, place tracing paper over the Vedic Square in Fig. 4.14 and mark a dot at the centre of each cell in which 1 appears. Join the six dots that result to obtain the 'shape' of 1. This is shown in Fig. 4.15a. Follow the same procedure for the number 8 to obtain Fig. 4.15b. Figs. 4.16–4.18 show the 'shapes' of the pairs of numbers 2 and 7, 3 and 6, and 4 and 5. The 'shape' of the number 9, shown in Figure 4.19 is unique. The last diagram, Fig. 4.20, is obtained by the superimposition of all the 'shapes' on a Vedic Square.

If we ignore the last row and column of 9s, a Vedic Square consists of a concentric ring of four squares, where the elements along each side of

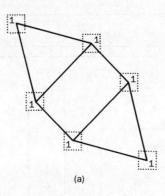

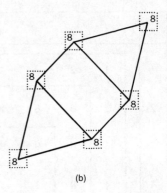

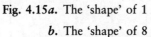

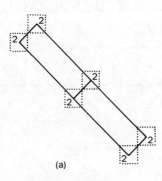

(a)   (b)

Fig. 4.15a. The 'shape' of 1
b. The 'shape' of 8

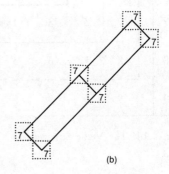

(a)   (b)

Fig. 4.16a. The 'shape' of 2
b. The 'shape' of 7

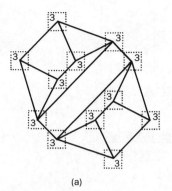
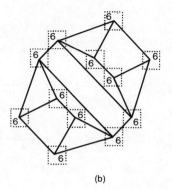

Fig. 4.17a. The 'shape' of 3
  b. The 'shape' of 6

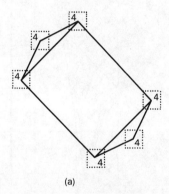
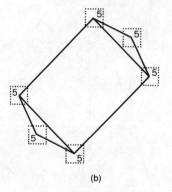

Fig. 4.18a. The 'shape' of 4
  b. The 'shape' of 5

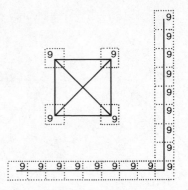

Fig. 4.19. The 'shape' of 9

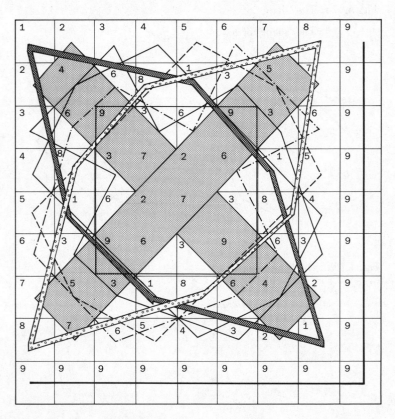

Fig. 4.20. The complete Vedic design

each square after carrying out the Vedic 'sum' (or adding the digits until a single digit is obtained) add up to 9. The innermost square in Fig. 4.14 contains the elements 2 and 7 along each side, whose sum equals 9. The 'shapes' of the numbers 2 and 7, as shown in Figs. 4.16*a* and *b*, indicate that one is a reflection of the other. In the next square the Vedic 'sum' of each side, consisting of the elements 9, 6, 3, and 9, is also 9. And the 'shapes' of the complements of 9, which in this instance consist of 3 and 6, are also reflections of one another, as shown in Figs. 4.17*a* and *b*. Similar reflection patterns exist between the 'shapes' of 1 and 8 and those of 4 and 5, as shown in Figs. 4.15*a* and *b* and 4.18*a* and *b*. The reader may also wish to check the fact that, with the exception of the 'shapes' of 2 and 7, the Vedic 'sum' of the numbers enclosed in each of the other figures all add to 9. The principle of reflection also means that, for each vertical column of numbers in the Vedic Square, there is an identical horizontal row of numbers. Thus, from the original multiplication table in Fig. 4.14 we are able to concretize certain abstract mathematical concepts such as like numbers (i.e. each pair of complements of 9), enclosure pairs, concentricity, reflective symmetry, and repetitions. These concepts are readily grasped by young children when they are talked through this example.

For older children, the same multiplication tables can introduce even subtler concepts. The appearance of the number 9 under all the guises discussed earlier could be a useful starting-point for a discussion of modular arithmetic. They could also be introduced to another form of transformation. A modular transformation is one in which each entry in Fig. 4.14 is divided by a chosen whole number, with the remainder becoming the new entry. Comparisons between a Remainder table and a Vedic table constructed with different divisors and bases would provide further insights into the shapes and patterns of numbers. For example, it is easily shown that a Vedic table of any base is identical to a Remainder table of the same base if the divisor used to obtain the remainders is 9.

In conclusion, it is interesting to note that students of arithmetic in ancient India were advised to study the complete Vedic design in Fig. 4.20 for a few minutes before attempting operations such as multiplication and division. Such a contemplation was supposed to improve their 'number sense' and thereby their efficiency as calculators.

5 Simultaneous Equations: A Numerical Approach from China

DAVID NELSON

A few years ago, three first-class and two second-class stamps cost 64 pence, while one first-class stamp and one second-class cost 25 pence. Can you say what single stamps of each class cost?

Two pieces of information and two unknown quantities to find—the price of each type of stamp.* Questions like this, and methods of dealing with them, have been a part of the mathematics curriculum for abler children for a long time. The reasons are not hard to find. It is natural to begin the science of unknown quantities with questions about one unknown, for example:

A quantity and one seventh of it added together become 19. What is the quantity? (Rhind Papyrus, 1650 BC, Egypt).

And it is natural to proceed to one or more statements about two unknowns. Babylonian tablets of 1600 BC contain such questions and Chapter 8 of the *Chiu Chang Suan Shu* (*Nine Chapters on the Mathematical Art* (first century BC, China)) is devoted to problems of the type given at the start of this chapter, some involving three or more unknowns. Here is an old problem from India:

The mixed price of 9 citrons and 7 fragrant wood apples is 107; again the mixture price of 7 citrons and 9 fragrant wood apples is 101. O you arithmetician, tell me quickly the price of a citron and of a wood apple here, having distinctly separated those prices well. (Mahavira, *c.* AD 850)

---

* For readers unfamiliar with the UK postal system, items sent first class are delivered quicker than those sent second class.

and here are Hall and Knight in their *Higher Algebra* (1897: 512):

209. In a mixed company consisting of Poles, Turks, Greeks, Germans and Italians, the Poles are one less than one-third of the number of Germans, and three less than half the number of Italians. The Turks and Germans outnumber the Greeks and Italians by 3; the Greeks and Germans form one less than half the company; while the Italians and Greeks form seven-sixteenths of the company: determine the number of each nation.

The modern curriculum tends to concentrate on:

1. linear and quadratic equations in one unknown, e.g.

$$3x + 5 = 11$$
$$x^2 + x = 20$$

2. simultaneous equations in two unknowns.

But it is worth noting that, historically, importance was placed on solving 'indeterminate' problems and equations—so called because they have an infinite number of solutions. An example of such a problem is:

Find a number which leaves remainder 6 when divided by 7 and 3 when divided by 5.

Its solution can be any number in the infinite list: . . . . −22, 13, 48, 83 . . .

A famous example of this type is Master Sun's (*c.* AD 280) problem—to find a number which leaves remainder 2, 3, and 2 when divided by 3, 5, and 7 respectively. It is likely that such problems were connected with calendar calculations, but the method of solution is of considerable mathematical interest and is called the Chinese Remainder Theorem in honour of Master Sun.

This is not the place to debate the absence of this type of problem from schoolwork, but there is no doubt they were studied seriously by the Greeks, Indians, and Chinese. Some circulated quite widely among ordinary people, often accompanied by names like 'the hundred fowls problem' or 'the Emperor Qin counting his soldiers secretly', and, in the case of Master Sun's problem, a rhyme concealing its solution.

To return to simultaneous equations, curiosity and the desire to extend one's powers are certainly motives for studying them. Competence in solving them is essential if one is to tackle problems of any complexity in science or mathematics where one has to work with more than one unknown quantity. But the topic suffers, like quadratic equations, from a serious drawback at the elementary level when it is considered for inclusion in the curriculum: when, in everyday life, do we come upon problems like these? We do not arrive at the prices of stamps or the cost of fruit by contemplating previous purchases. It is difficult to find occasions when one has used simultaneous equations in the home. I can give just two instances:

1. finding a satisfactory mixture of heights for the shelves of a three-shelf bookcase of fixed overall height;
2. working out with my wife how to lose a given number of stitches from a row of knitting by means of a suitable mixture of 'knit 3', 'knit 2 together', and 'knit 4'.

By contrast, it is easy to find practical instances of equations in one unknown. Adapting the Rhind Papyrus problem we quoted earlier to modern times one has:

The cost of an article together with a 15% value added tax is £19. What was the original cost?

So, if simultaneous equations are included in the school curriculum, they will, in the early stages, arise from problems with an artificial ring to them. The examples quoted earlier in the chapter suggest this may have been the case from the beginning. One of the earliest collections of such problems is the eighth chapter of the *Nine Chapters on the Mathematical Art*. Whereas some of the problems elsewhere in that book deal with practical questions such as the areas of fields or the quantity of earth required for an embankment of a certain shape, no pretence at reality is to be found in Chapter 8. The first problem (involving three unknowns) begins:

'The yield of 3 sheaves of superior grain, 2 sheaves of medium grain, and 1 sheaf of inferior grain is 39 *tou*.* The yield of . . .'

* The grain measure 1 *tou* = 10 *sheng* ≏ 2 litres in the Han period.

Examples like this remind us that at times curiosity, or the cultivation of a technique without regard to its immediate applicability, has been a driving force in separate developments of mathematics in different cultures. So also has been recreational pleasure. One finds Brahmagupta posing problems 'simply for pleasure' and the command 'solve' is replaced by enticing invitations, such as: 'Say, intelligent calculator . . .', 'Tell me, most enchanting lady . . .', or even 'O you who are clever in miscellaneous problems on fractions, give . . .'

The main aims of this chapter are to discuss the method for solving equations given in the Chinese *Nine Chapters* and to explore whether it might be transferred to the present-day classroom.

Let us recall the problem given at the start of the chapter:

A few years ago, three first-class and two second-class stamps cost 64 pence, while one first-class and one second-class cost 25 pence; can you say what single stamps of each class cost?

A popular contemporary method of solution is as follows:

1. Let x and y be the cost of a first-class and second-class stamp.
2. Translate the above 'word problem' into symbolic form (A):

$$3x + 2y = 64$$
$$x + y = 25$$

3. Double the sides of the second equation:

$$3x + 2y = 64$$
$$2x + 2y = 50$$

and then subtract each side of the second equation from the corresponding side of the first. This gives

$$x = 14$$

and then

$$y = 11$$

4. Translate this solution back into 'word' form: a first-class stamp costs 14 pence, a second-class stamp costs 11 pence.

The approach in *Nine Chapters* is essentially as follows:

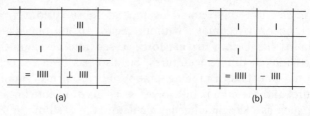

Fig. 5.1*a*.

b.

1. Set up a table (B):

First	Second	Cost
3	2	64
1	1	25

2. Twice subtract the second row from the first:

1	0	14
1	1	25

3. State the solution: a first-class stamp costs 14 pence, a second-class stamp costs 11 pence.

In actual fact the problem was set up in columns rather than rows. So using the rod numeral system described in Chapter 3, the two tables above would have been set out as Fig. 5.1*a* and *b*. But, for convenience, we will use rows for our equations and modern decimal notation.

It is tempting to suggest that the Chinese interest and expertise in this type of problem was fuelled by the readiness with which it could be transferred to and worked on their 'counting boards'. The technique was known as 'the method of square tables'.

Comparing the two approaches, we see that in both cases the solver is thinking in terms of unknowns, such as 'the cost of a first-class stamp', but the second approach cuts out the use of letters x and y for unknowns. Abstraction is present, but it is mental rather than mental and symbolic. Thus the table B lacks the algebraic symbolism of the equations A; the solver does not have to construct an expression such as $3x + 2y$ and equate it to 64. (Incidentally, if negative quantities had been involved, they would have been indicated in the Chinese solution by the use of counting rods of a different colour, the convention being red for positive, black for negative (unlike Western banks!).) Finally, the manipulative strategy in the Chinese method (the *fang cheng*) is identical to the Western method of elimination by addition and subtraction of equations. Namely, the aim is to get a zero in a row for one of the unknowns. In the case of problems with three unknowns, the aim is for two zeros in one row and one zero in one other. It is thought that this method, usually called 'Gaussian elimination' or 'reduction to row-echelon form', was first developed in the West by the French mathematician Jean Buteo ($c.1492$–$c.1572$) in the sixteenth century. In this form it is economical on computing time and still one of the best available methods for solving such problems (see Higham 1991).

To the teacher introducing children to simultaneous equations the Chinese approach has a number of attractions.

1. The essential processes are the same. The pupil will have nothing to unlearn when moving on to the algebraic method of solution later.

2. It avoids, for the moment, the pressure of algebraic symbolism. Children can find the transition from 'verbal' or 'mental' algebra to formal symbolic algebra difficult. It takes practice and experience to become fluent and confident in translating a 'word problem' into a symbolic form such as A.

3. Manipulating rows of numbers in a table seems a more tangible and tractable affair than working with terms or 'sides' of equations. This gain in 'concreteness' may be all important for success with weaker pupils.

Later in this chapter I shall describe a lesson illustrating how the approach might be introduced in the classroom. The lesson lasted seventy minutes and was given to thirteen-year-olds of slightly above average ability in one of Manchester's inner city mixed comprehensive schools. The main aim was to introduce the Chinese method and use it. A subsidiary aim was to introduce the Chinese rod numeral system and become familiar with it.

A fortnight before the lesson, in order to get to know the children

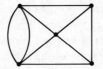

Fig. 5.2

Fig. 5.3

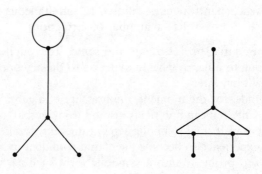

Fig. 5.4

and work with them a little, I visited the school with a student teacher. Together we investigated whether there are laws connecting the numbers of nodes, arcs, and regions in connected networks, such as those shown in Fig. 5.2 (5 nodes, 9 arcs, 6 regions), and Fig. 5.3 (7 nodes, 6 arcs, 1 region), and then whether there are laws when we have two networks on the page, as in Fig. 5.4 (10 nodes, 10 arcs, 3 regions) and so on. (The children were already familiar with simple algebraic ideas.) By the end of an animated class the consensus was that, if we had a number (*n*), of separate networks then

1. nodes plus regions minus arcs comes to one more than the number of networks, or

2. $$N + R - A = 1 + n$$

In the light of our remarks in Chapter 2 about the development of algebra, it was interesting to see that the children tended to declare their results in the rhetorical form (1) or a symbolic compromise between (1) and (2) rather than use the purely symbolic form (2).

Whereas the traceability (in one sweep of the pen or finger) of a network has interested non-European cultures (see the Shongo diagrams of Chapter 6), the above relation and its analogue for polyhedra (vertices + faces − edges = 2) appears to be exclusively European, and so we praised the class for rediscovering a theorem of the eighteenth-century Swiss mathematician Euler.

After this successful attempt to find and state an algebraic formula, it was not hard to return and offer an excursion into Chinese mathematics as a reward. The preliminary lesson had been investigative and largely pupil-led. The main lesson was teacher-led—its chief aims being to do some Chinese arithmetic and then some algebra.

I began by unfurling a world map, asking for the position and population of China. The single Chinese child in the class showed us where his relations lived. After agreeing that the population of China is around 1000 million, we compared it with that of the United Kingdom—a difference of 950 million, a ratio of 20 : 1, the UK population being 5 per cent of the size of China's. We could have talked of land areas or the numbers of Chinese resident in Manchester or the United Kingdom. The scope for animated numerate discussion was considerable.

Next we looked at the way they used to write their numbers with rod numerals, or display them on a counting board with rods. The system is decimal but has two sets of symbols for the digits 1–9: one for the units, hundreds, ten thousands, etc., places, and one for the tens, thousands, etc., places (see Fig. 3.3).

We quickly worked three exercises. The first turned numbers like 1987 into Chinese; the second turned numbers like ⊤⊺ o ⏐ into decimal notation; the third asked 'Why do you think the Chinese used a different set of numerals for the tens and units place?' This drew answers like: 'so that you don't get vertical lines next to vertical lines or horizontal lines next to horizontal lines and to stop the confusion', and 'to stop confusion when someone knocked the board'.

After this easy task it seemed important to put the children's knowledge to more profitable use, and they looked at copies of either the Chu Shih-chieh triangle of 1303 (Fig. 5.5) or the 1781 Japanese version of Murai (Fig. 5.6). In each case they were asked to translate into modern notation. The Chinese text presents difficulties because the diagram is meant to be read lying on its side (Needham (1959: 137) suggests reasons for this). Also, as the children were quick to point out, the rule about using two sets of symbols is not always obeyed. The Japanese text is easier to translate and has the advantage of containing below the triangle an explanation of the rule of formation of the pattern of numbers. The introduction of original texts into the classroom was clearly stimulating.

Thirty minutes were spent on this part of the lesson and, after an impromptu quiz on the then current colour and value of first-class and second-class stamps (green, 18p; brown, 13p), the following puzzle was introduced:

If one knew that, a few years ago, two firsts and four seconds cost 72p, and a first and second together cost 25p, what did single stamps of each type cost?

At this point a graphic form of the problem was displayed, with green and brown rectangles to represent stamps (see Fig. 5.7). Various methods (including trial and error) were suggested for solving the problem. The most popular was to remove a pair of first-class and a pair of second-class stamps from the top row and reduce the cost by 50p, thus leaving two second-class stamps with a cost of 22p. This meant a second-class stamp was worth 11p and, looking at the bottom row, we saw a first-class stamp was worth 14p. To be sure we had not made a slip we checked that this solution also fitted the top row of the original diagram. I explained that this was similar to the way the Chinese would have set out and solved this sort of problem almost two thousand years ago. We agreed to write our solutions on squared paper instead

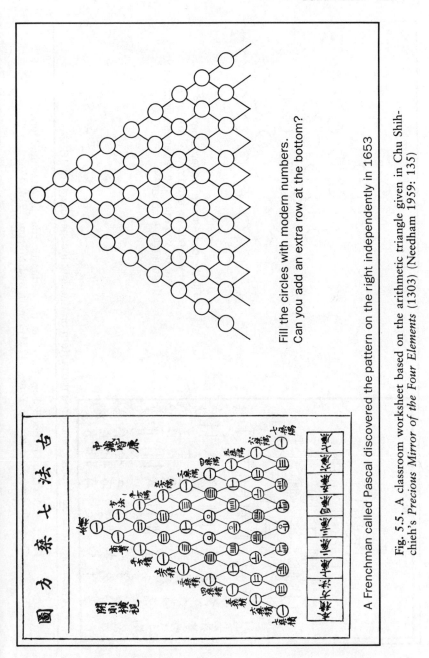

Fill the circles with modern numbers.
Can you add an extra row at the bottom?

A Frenchman called Pascal discovered the pattern on the right independently in 1653

Fig. 5.5. A classroom worksheet based on the arithmetic triangle given in Chu Shih-chieh's *Precious Mirror of the Four Elements* (1303) (Needham 1959: 135)

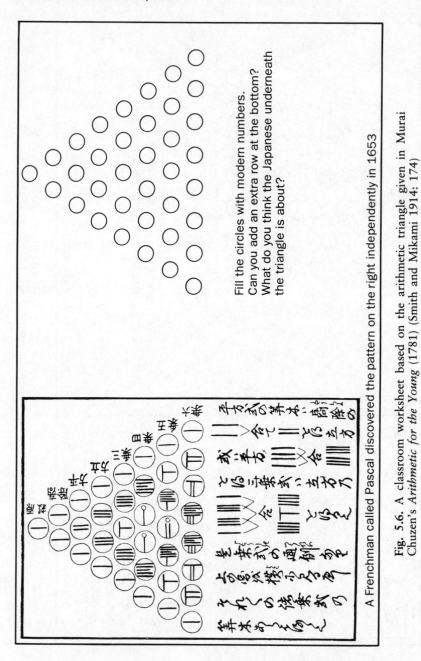

Fill the circles with modern numbers.
Can you add an extra row at the bottom?
What do you think the Japanese underneath
the triangle is about?

A Frenchman called Pascal discovered the pattern on the right independently in 1653

Fig. 5.6. A classroom worksheet based on the arithmetic triangle given in Murai Chuzen's *Arithmetic for the Young* (1781) (Smith and Mikami 1914: 174)

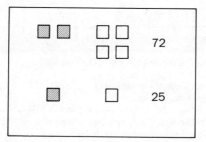

Fig. 5.7

of a counting board, using modern numerals rather than rod numerals.

First	Second	Cost
2	4	72
1	1	25
2	4	72
2	2	50
0	2	22
2	2	50
1 second costs		11
1 first costs		14

Of course this was only one of several schemes proposed. Others were 'multiply the second row by four and subtract the first row', and 'subtract the second row from the first until a zero appears', and in practice some children preferred to give the solution in a table:

0	1	11
1	0	14

We tried a second problem together and spent the remainder of the class consolidating the skill with examples. The first four were

Table 5.1. Lesson plan

Activities or Content	Time
World map, China's population, 1000 million Chinese rod numeral system Exercise and feedback of answers Texts to translate and discuss	30
Quiz on first-class and second-class stamps	5

Problem
  2 firsts 4 seconds 72p
  1 first 1 second 25p
Discuss solution
Agree a model for written solutions
	15

Exercises and personal tuition	15
Review and conclude lesson	5

Ideas involved
  ratio, percentage
  a number system
  a number pattern
  simultaneous equations solved by elimination	

about stamps, then fruit, chess, and fruit. Here, for the reader to try, are the last two.

At chess 2 bishops and 1 castle are worth 11 pawns. Also 1 bishop and 2 castles are worth 13 pawns. What is the value of a castle in pawns? What is the value of a bishop?

Three girls bought some fruit at a market stall. Ann bought 1 orange, 1 lemon, and 2 apples for 36p. Mary bought 1 orange, 2 lemons, and 3 apples for 55p. Usha bought 2 oranges, 3 lemons, and 1 apple for 55p. What were the prices of single oranges, lemons, and apples at that stall?

One of the pupils almost completed the solution to this final question, but made an arithmetic error. Everyone successfully solved at least three problems in the fifteen minutes available. Table 5.1 gives the plan for the lesson and a list of some of the ideas involved. The Chinese method has been tried on other occasions. A student teacher gave low-attaining twelve-year-olds prepared arrays to solve and was surprised at the success rates achieved.

As well as introducing the method before the algebraic method, it can be introduced (or reintroduced) *after* the algebraic method has been studied. Sixth-formers solving equations in three unknowns found the Chinese numerical approach labour-saving and advantageous. In fact, it is advocated in some textbooks.

Li Yan and Du Shiran (1988) or Needham (1959) provide opportunities to look at other achievements of Chinese algebra and decide whether or not some could assist mathematics education. One could begin by looking at three themes.

1. Another way in which the Chinese used the counting board to record and manipulate algebraic expressions was 'the technique of the celestial element', in which columns of numbers such as

$$
\begin{array}{ccc}
3 & & \\
2 & & \\
6 & \text{and} & 3 \\
1 & & 2
\end{array}
$$

stood for

$$3x^3 + 2x^2 + 6x + 1 \qquad \text{and} \qquad 3x + 2$$

This is worth considering as an aid to multiplying or dividing these expressions. The product can be conveniently set out (in rows) as follows:

	3	2	6	1
			3	2
	6	4	12	2
9	6	18	3	
9	12	22	15	2

the answer being

$$9x^4 + 12x^3 + 22x^2 + 15x + 2$$

The method is known in the West as 'detached coefficients', but has been neglected.

2. Working as above with just the coefficients, by the thirteenth century the Chinese perfected methods for extracting roots* and solving higher-degree equations by a stepwise (iterative) process. Their first methods for extracting roots used what we call Pascal's triangle and the diagram in Fig. 5.5 was 'the source of the method of extracting roots'. A later method applicable to extracting roots

e.g. $$\sqrt[4]{1336336}$$

but also solving equations

e.g. $$-5x^4 + 52x^3 + 128x^2 = 4096$$

does not require the triangle. It was called 'extracting roots by iterated multiplication' and is identical to the nineteenth-century Ruffini–Horner method (Ruffini 1804, Horner 1819). The method is simple, almost automatic, and tedious, for after a few steps the calculation tends to involve very large numbers. Faster and more efficient methods are now available. Nevertheless it is fascinating to find such ingenuity and painstaking calculation taking place eight hundred years before it was discovered in the West.

3. The *fang cheng* method applies to linear equations. It does not apply to the problem of finding the sides x, y of a rectangle whose area is 20 and perimeter is 24:

$$\text{i.e.} \qquad \left.\begin{array}{r} xy = 20 \\ x + y = 12 \end{array}\right\}$$

However, the Chinese did develop special methods for dealing with such problems, and, by the thirteenth century, Chu Shih-chieh in *The Precious Mirror of the Four Elements* (1303) showed how to use the counting board to record and manipulate algebraic expressions in up to four variables (heaven, earth, human, and material). It involved allocating to the holes of the grid (and some of its intersections) various combinations of the variables. If we call the variables x, y, z, u, part of the allocation is as shown in Fig. 5.8, and Fig. 5.9 represented $2u + uz + xz + 3xu$. Note the 大 (*tai*) to mark the central position. This was the 'constant term' to which the expession was set equal.

---

* Finding square roots, cube roots, etc.

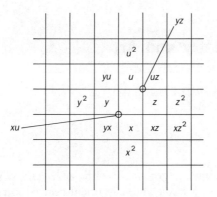

Fig. 5.8

Fig. 5.9. $2u + uz + xz + 3xu$

In spite of the skill with which these diagrams were used, the limitations of the notation are plain: (*a*) cross terms such as xu^2 and x^2u will be difficult to locate; (*b*) there is no place for products such as xyz in this scheme; (*c*) we are limited to four unknowns. So this theme offers, on the one hand, a graphic way of illustrating expressions in more than one variable, and, on the other, a notational cul de sac.

The main aim of this chapter has been to discuss and give some precise details of a cultural approach to the topic of simultaneous equations. It is fitting, however, that the momentum of the discussion carried us into three further areas—polynomial algebra, iterative solutions of equations, and alternative algebraic notations—for it has touched on the remarkable achievements of Chinese algebra and the strengths and limitations of an algebra based on a computational aid: the counting board.

6 Geometry and Art

JULIAN WILLIAMS

What has 'geometry' got to do with 'art'? And why are we discussing them in a book about multicultural education?

The connection between geometry and art lies in their common interest in space. Geometry is about the mathematical analysis of points and lines and shapes in space, while art is often concerned with aesthetic appreciation or with the use of space to evoke an emotional response. In some cases art can be thought of as an application of geometry. Certainly there are schools or branches of art in which geometrical principles are central to the construction of the drawing or design.

We are quite used to the idea of mathematics being useful because of its applications in science and technology. However, even in commercial terms, art and 'good design' are increasingly seen as being as important as science and 'good engineering' to an artefact or system, and as an essential element to bridge the traditional divide between technologists, who can make things that work, and artists, who can make things that look elegant. It is clearly a sound principle to bring together technology and art, or utility and elegance, in design and manufacture.

It is, therefore, a priority for educationalists to find ways to bridge the divide between science and art in schools. This must impinge on the mathematics curriculum. Just as we have learnt that computers are as important to the artist as to the scientist, so we must learn how *mathematics* is as useful to art as it is to science.

But there are deeper educational reasons motivating a concern for the linking of mathematics and art. The geometry involved in art and design can be much more accessible and enjoyable to most students than the mathematics involved in scientific applications.

For many of us, mathematics may have more *personal* value because of its application in art and design. The shapers of the mathematics curriculum are often wont to refer to the needs of society, the demands of industry, and the requirements of everyday adult life. The other crucial element in curriculum design, however, which this approach often ignores, is the immediate needs of the pupil. The average student needs emotional and intellectual satisfaction now, and not just in five or ten years' time, when they become adults! The pleasure and satisfaction that children find in drawing, in colour, and in modelling can, perhaps, contribute to their learning of mathematics. And the development of geometrical concepts and skills can be applied to help the child or student gain pleasure from creative art. If we can achieve this, the child will appreciate the relevance and the power of mathematics in a personal way, and will associate the pleasure of creative art with that of creative mathematics.

But what of the multicultural connection? The multicultural connection lies in the naturally multicultural context of art. In particular, in this chapter, we choose to look at the geometry of two-dimensional patterns and designs. Art of this kind is found all over the world, in brickwork, woodwork, tiles, weaving, carpets, and works of art. Arabic geometrical designs have perhaps the most developed and sophisticated tradition in this respect, but many of these designs are found in ancient India, China, and Africa and, of course, have been integrated into modern Western culture. It has been impossible to ascribe a precise historical trajectory to the transmission of these designs and patterns, though we shall give existing sources of some designs in this chapter. What is important, educationally, is that the student should gain an appreciation of their artistic and mathematical beauty, whether or not they are part of that student's traditional culture. Our studies should include as wide a variety of cultural sources as possible, so that the student should enjoy a rich experience. And we should make the sources explicitly known to the student so as to enlighten him as to the rich contribution that other cultures make. In this way, we may achieve some of the aims of the curriculum for mathematics and art, while also educating for a multicultural society. In a national curriculum, such as is used in England and Wales, which has no specific objectives relating to

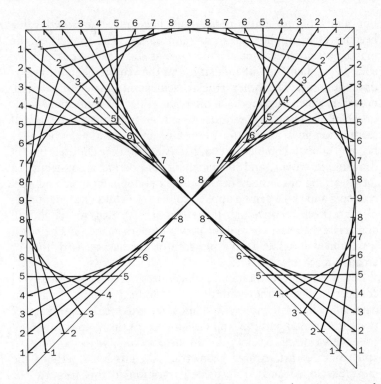

Fig. 6.1. A design produced by drawing line segments between pairs of numbers which add up to 10

multicultural education, this is a necessary approach; but it is, in any case, a desirable one.

Let us consider, by way of illustration, a practical example. A primary teacher may wish to provide an exercise on number bonds, thus leading to achievement of mathematical objectives. She may also wish to stimulate some artistic activity through curve-stitching. Finally, it is 17 March and she may wish to tell the children of the legend of St Patrick and the religious meaning of the shamrock, thereby informing their understanding of another culture. Fig. 6.1 shows an activity designed for the purpose. You may have some reservations about this example of multicultural mathematics, but let us first examine its merits.

First, the pattern of the number bonds is reflected in the pattern of lines which it generates, thus giving strong visual support to an important numerical relationship. In particular, the emerging geometric pattern provides a self-checking mechanism for the pupil, so that a mistake such as 5 + 4 = 10 should be spotted and corrected. The final shape of the shamrock emerges as a surprise to the uninitiated child, and is a reward for concentration and skill.

Secondly, the act of drawing may itself be pleasurable, and provide a contrast to the repetitive recall of number bonds. The child may be made aware of the possibility of using the curve-stitching technique for creating his or her own designs, patterns, and pictures, providing an open-ended, creative activity to follow on.

Thirdly, the making of the shamrock provides a cultural link for the teacher to exploit. Children of Irish background may tell the class about St Patrick, and the nature of the Holy Trinity may be introduced and discussed.

These mathematical and motivational points constitute a strong case for using curve-stitching with children of an appropriate age; it is, in fact, a very popular activity in many classrooms. It is the multicultural dimension which interests us here. There is a certain artificiality about the emergence of the shamrock, since the same technique could equally well be used to generate other signs and symbols. The discussion of St Patrick and the Holy Trinity does seem here to be a diversion from the essence of the activity as it was experienced by the children when they did it. One wonders whether a more coherent and valid follow-up by the teacher and pupils might not focus on the questions about mathematics or art involved:

1. Can you use straight lines to generate other 'envelope' curves?
2. What patterns would you get from different number bonds?
3. Can you make a picture using this technique?

And it might be argued that a more appropriate introduction to St Patrick's Day would be for the teacher to ask the children if they know why she is wearing a shamrock to school today.

These are essentially criticisms which apply generally to the prevalent 'topic' approach in many schools, i.e. that the activities which are subsumed under the topic often bear little more than a token relationship to each other. It is not unfair to say that most attempts at the multicultural approach to mathematics do suffer from tokenism. Having told a class that the word 'algebra' has an Arabic origin, a teacher is likely to proceed to teach algebra for three years without further reference to culture, however willing and positively inclined to multiculturalism he or she may be.

Note that the link between mathematics and art in the curve-stitching is *not* a token one; it is, in fact, quite genuine and natural. It is the introduction of the multicultural element which seems forced. If, however, curve-stitching was seen as essentially Irish, in the same sense as Gaelic football is, then I think this objection would dissolve.

Thus, if we develop the link between mathematics and the art of a variety of cultures then we will have a genuine and natural vehicle for educating children in these cultures through mathematics. For example, the Arabic tradition in patterns and designs provides an ideal context for work in geometry and art. It would not be an exaggeration to say that the entire school geometry curriculum could be introduced and applied through the study of Islamic patterns. The bulk of this chapter will show how some of this can be done. The power of the approach lies in the proposition that the mathematics enables the child to create art. This fact will be enough to motivate children, and, hence, to motivate their teachers to adopt the approach.

The multicultural significance lies in the fact that the cultural source is *central* rather than token. The result of appropriate instruction for the child might be, for example, that he or she is encouraged to create a design which might be appropriate for the doors of a mosque, or at least to appreciate the artistic and mathematical merits of someone else's Islamic design! Such an approach is a rational one, it seems to me, in giving a child respect and admiration for the achievements of his or her own culture, and of the cultures of other peoples.

Before we proceed to some case studies, let us outline some of the principal stages in the school geometry curriculum, and how these might be applied in the study of a traditional Arabic design (Fig. 6.2a) or a Chinese lattice (Fig. 6.2b).

Broadly, the development of children's geometrical thinking between the ages of five and sixteen falls into three stages. The

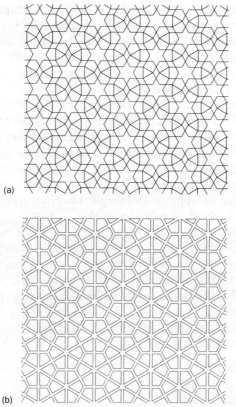

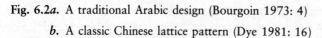

Fig. 6.2a. A traditional Arabic design (Bourgoin 1973: 4)

   b. A classic Chinese lattice pattern (Dye 1981: 16)

first stage consists mainly of the recognition, naming, and use of the common geometric objects, particularly the two- and three-dimensional shapes. This involves drawing shapes such as squares and triangles in pictures and diagrams, being able to select appropriate shapes to make a pattern, and discussing shapes and their position using appropriate language.

This is one occasion when a colouring activity, often scorned as a time-filler for young children, really has merit. Selecting a colour for and colouring in each different shape in Fig. 6.2a involve discrimination and recognition of shapes entirely appropriate to this stage. Also at this stage it is appropriate to select or make tiles to build up a pattern, as in Fig. 6.2b. Children may be asked to cut out kites of appropriate shape, say from triangular dotted paper, to tile the design in Fig. 6.2b.

Also at this stage, it is appropriate to hunt for various shapes in a pattern, or to draw as many different shapes as you can find. For example, in Fig. 6.2b there are kites, triangles, hexagons, rhombuses (diamonds), parallelograms, trapeziums, irregular pentagons, and many other shapes to be found. Such an activity can be very demanding, as it can involve extracting a figure from a 'noisy' background of distracting lines. In the Arabic design, Fig. 6.2a, for instance, can you find

1. a hexagon?
2. a space rocket?
3. a radiation warning sign?

During this first stage, the *Gestalt* recognition of shapes and the language of position, shape, and size are developed and used. Children do not *explicitly* or consciously know about the properties of shapes or how they fit together, but they develop an ability to sort and discriminate perceptually.

At the next stage, the second stage of development, children's practical activity with shape and their discussion of their findings develop a conscious knowledge of the properties of shapes. The numbers of sides, size of angles, and symmetry of figures all become the object of experiment and discovery.

Investigating the Chinese lattice design in Fig. 6.2b for shapes which tessellate, we find equilateral triangles, hexagons, parallelograms, rhombuses, kites, and trapeziums. It appears, in fact, that

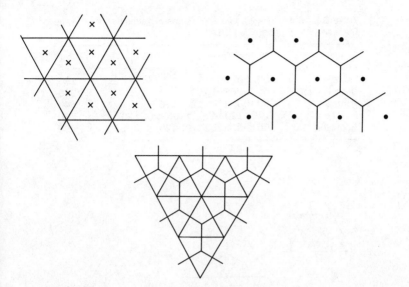

Fig. 6.3. Triangular and hexagonal lattices overlaid to generate the Chinese lattice design

the pattern might be thought of as being generated by two overlapping tessellations. Take transparencies of a tessellation of triangles, and of hexagons, and then overlay them (see Fig. 6.3).

Investigating the angles and angle-sums of the various polygons in the design follow very simply from knowing the angles of the kite, i.e. 60°, 90°, 120°, 90°. Children can collect results on the various shapes and list their findings, as shown in Table 6.1. It should be noted that the angle-sum increases each time by 180°. Such an investigation is commonplace in secondary-school geometry. In this context, the enquiry is especially simple, because the angles are all multiples of 30°.

It should also be noted that there are examples of many *different* (but similar) polygons of each type. Examining the triangles in the lattice, one finds only equilateral triangles, consisting of 3, 12, 27, 48 kites respectively. Thus, the triangles are similar in length ratio 1 : 2 : 3 : 4 and in area ratio 1 : 4 : 9 : 16 (see Fig. 6.4).

A similar situation arises for other symmetric figures. There are rhombuses in the length ratio 1 : 2 : 3 : 4 and area ratio 1 : 4 : 9 : 16; similarly parallelograms and trapeziums. This leads to the obser-

Table 6.1. Interior angles and angle-sums of various shapes in the Chinese lattice pattern, Fig. 6.2*b*

Shape	Angles (degrees)	Total
Triangle	60, 60, 60	180
Quadrilateral	60, 90, 90, 120	360
Pentagon	90, 90, 120, 120, 120	540
Hexagon	120, 120, 120, 120, 120, 120	720
Heptagon	60, 60, 120, 120, 120, 120, 300	900

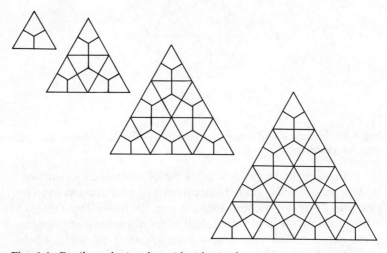

Fig. 6.4. Equilateral triangles with sides in the ratio $1:2:3:4$ and areas, measured by the numbers of tiles, in the ratio $3:12:27:48$ or $1:4:9:16$

vation that area ratios are the squares of length ratios. For regular hexagons a curious situation arises, for we have a regular hexagon of area 6 kites and another of area 18 kites. So it appears we have an area ratio of $1:3$, which is consistent with a length ratio of $1:\sqrt{3}$. Indeed, application of trigonometry shows that this is the case, since the lengths of the sides of the kite are in the ratio $\cos 60° : \sin 60°$, or $\frac{1}{2} : \frac{\sqrt{3}}{2}$ or $1:\sqrt{3}$ (see Fig. 6.5).

The situation with quadrilaterals is different. We can find and classify a number of dissimilar quadrilaterals; kites, rhombuses, parallelograms, and trapeziums. It is possible to investigate their

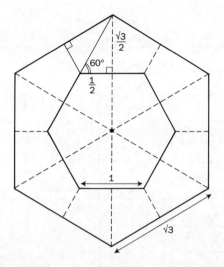

Fig. 6.5. Area and length ratio of two hexagons: the lengths of the sides of the kite are in the ratio cos 60° : sin 60°, or $1 : \sqrt{3}$, consistent with an area ratio of $1:3$

angles or areas as above, but it is also evident that they may be classified according to such properties as number of pairs of equal sides, number of pairs of parallel sides, order of symmetry, or number of lines of symmetry. Children may group the shapes into tables according to their number of pairs of equal sides and pairs of parallel sides; alternatively shapes can be tabulated according to their number of lines of symmetry and order of rotational symmetry (see Fig. 6.6).

One is inclined to ask why there are blanks in some of the cells of the matrix. Is it because there are no shapes in this particular lattice which happen to fit, or is it that there are no quadrilaterals whatsoever that could fit into these cells? Such thinking is characteristic of the higher stage of reasoning and reflection involved in the next stage, i.e. the third stage.

At the third stage, the child should begin to order the experimental discoveries of the second stage and appreciate that certain properties of shapes are related. We expect an appreciation of the idea that shapes satisfy general rules: for instance, a regular *n*-sided

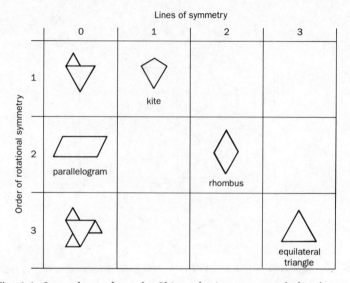

Fig. 6.6. Some shapes from the Chinese lattice pattern, tabulated according to their symmetries

polygon must *always* have n equal angles totalling $(n - 2) \times 180°$. We explore the reasons for these general rules. Algebraic generalization is not always necessary for reasoning at this stage. Consider the rules for angles and parallel lines or for congruent triangles, for instance. While the processes involved at the second stage are predominantly: 'What properties does this shape have?' or 'Can I find a shape which has . . .', at the third stage there is a new level of thought process: 'These shapes must have this property because . . .' or 'There is no such shape because . . .'

It is also characteristic of the latter, higher stages of geometrical thinking that the child begins to think formally, i.e. to use formal procedures for analysing, describing, and deducing. Examples of this will become clearer if we describe the procedural approach to creating designs.

Starting at an arbitrary kite marked 0 in the Chinese lattice of Fig. 6.7, we can rotate it clockwise about A through multiples of 60°: R_1, R_2, R_3, R_4, R_5; these rotations move the kite to the positions labelled 1, 2, 3, 4, 5. We note that a further 60° rotation gets the kite back to zero, and that to go from 0 to 3 or from 1

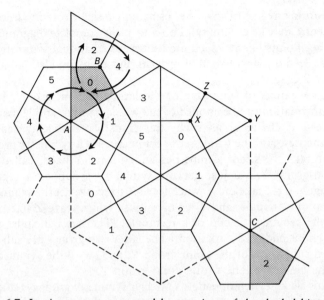

Fig. 6.7. Lattice pattern generated by rotations of the shaded kite at *A*

to 4 represents a 180° rotation, R_3. Rotating the kite about a different centre, *B*, by multiples of 120°, we label new kites 2 and 4. Note that every time we rotate clockwise we *add* the appropriate number, +1 for a 60° rotation, +2 for a 120° rotation, etc. Subject to the requirement that all answers more than 5 are reduced by appropriate multiples of 6 so that 2 + 4 = 0, 3 + 5 = 2, 4 + 4 = 2, we can proceed to label each kite in the figure (see Fig. 6.7). So, in Fig. 6.7, each kite of the lattice is labelled according to the angle of rotation required to rotate the shaded kite on to it.

Now we have formally assigned a number to each kite in the entire design, we can deduce the rotation required to get any kite to any other kite! There may, however, be a need for a translation as well, for example, to map the shaded kite at *A* to that at *C* involves a translation along the line *AC*, then a 120° rotation about *C*. Here is a challenge, though: you can get there directly using only a single 120° rotation without the need for a translation.

In general, according to an important theorem, it is possible to transform any kite to any other using only a single rotation (though its centre may be at infinity). Looking at the complete diagram, we can see points like X which are centres of rotational symmetry of order 3, and points like Y of order 6. But there are also points of order 2, like Z.

These points of symmetry of the lattice form a 'group'. Each transformation can be applied to the whole pattern, and leaves the pattern unchanged; as such, the transformations are called symmetries, and the whole set of symmetries is a symmetry group. If we take the set of symmetries which leave Y fixed, called the point group Y, we just get the symmetry group of a regular hexagon. If we take those which leave X fixed, we get the symmetry group of a triangle, and if we take those which leave Z fixed, we get the symmetry group of a rectangle! (The latter includes two reflections and a 180° rotation.) The latter two groups are subsets, called subgroups of the point group Y, and so all the symmetries of the pattern belong to the point group Y.

This classification of patterns by their symmetry groups is studied by crystallographers, and can be pursued through multicultural sources of pattern and design. Zaslavsky (1973) reproduces a picture of embroidered cloths from Kuba, Zaïre (now in the British Museum), which provides a complete set of seven different one-dimensional strip patterns. These patterns involve transformations in one dimension, such as 180° rotations and horizontal and vertical reflections.

Group theory has been used to prove that only seven such patterns can exist. The formal deduction of these results on symmetry groups and their subgroups would complete the development of the third stage of geometric thinking. This is beyond school geometry. Most students at school can go some way towards this, however; they can, for example, appreciate that any pattern with two perpendicular reflectional symmetries must have a rotational symmetry of order 2. Fig. 6.8 shows two strip patterns with rotational symmetry of order 2, but only one of these has horizontal and vertical lines of symmetry.

Note that the Chinese, Arabic, and African examples given for each geometrical stage have been *descriptive*. Each activity involves recognizing mathematics in the design, or analysing and describing the design mathematically. In no sense have we gone so

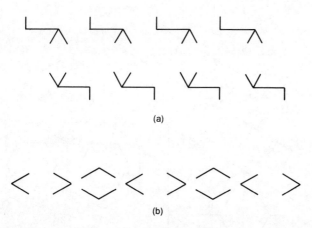

(a)

(b)

Fig. 6.8a. Rotational symmetry of order 2, without horizontal or vertical line symmetry

    b. Rotational symmetry of order 2, as well as horizontal and vertical line symmetry

far as to fulfil our programme as initially set out, i.e. to show how mathematics can be used to *create* a design. I hope, however, that the activities so far described are nevertheless of value.

It would still be fair to ask of these activities, what does art add to the mathematics of the activity, and in what sense do the activities achieve multicultural objectives? It is clear that most of the foregoing activities with shapes could be done with *any* collection of shapes. The advantages of restricting the activity to a narrow selection of shapes would still be there in a lattice design such as the triangular lattice. The only advantage to be had is from the, perhaps minor, motivating factor of studying a *real* and *attractive* design.

Furthermore, the cultural origin of the design may have minimal or minor significance to the mathematics of the activity. Similar designs of African, Indian, or even Western origin can give contexts for the same activities. There are books available (e.g. Wade 1982) with examples of such designs from all over the globe. It is difficult to attribute most of these beautiful designs to any one culture. Is this advantageous or disadvantageous to our multicultural objectives?

What about our ambitious objective of creating art and design

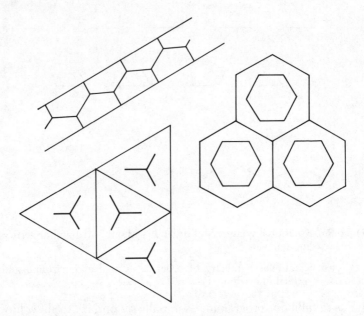

Fig. 6.9. Three designs obtained by shading and colouring the Chinese lattice pattern

using mathematics? In fact, it is not a very big step to go from describing a design to creating new designs. What is required is that we describe a procedure for generating the particular design, and then transfer or generalize it.

At the most basic level, one can describe the Chinese lattice design as a tessellation of kites, made by taking many kite tiles and fitting them together by trial and error. A trial-and-error procedure will, of course, work for many shapes and requires little mathematical knowledge.

Finding various shapes in the lattice, such as hexagons, trapeziums, pentagons, and parallelograms, readily leads to drawing new patterns. The children may either replace some kites in the mosaic by another shape, or can colour kites together to make new patterns explicit in the lattice. All the designs in Fig. 6.9 are obtained by shading and colouring the lattice in Fig. 6.2*b*.

I observed previously that the lattice can be thought of as the result of a two-step procedure:

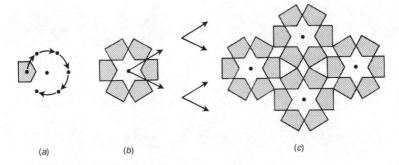

(a)   (b)   (c)

Fig. 6.10. Generating the Arabic design in Fig. 6.2*a*

1. drawing a lattice (i.e. of triangles);
2. overlaying the lattice of centres (hexagons generated by the centres of the triangles).

In fact, taking any tessellation, we can generate a similar design using the same procedure. A generating procedure for the Arabic design in Fig. 6.2*a* is less easy to find. One solution involves taking a pentagon (Fig. 6.10*a*), rotating it six times to form a flower-shape with a six-pointed star inside it (Fig. 6.10*b*), then tessellating the flower by translating it to the centres of other stars which then form a rhombic lattice (Fig. 6.10*c*). Alternatively, the pentagon can be rotated three times about the centre of the triangle. Then successive rotations or reflections of the triangular element will generate the pattern.

Let us now examine two more tessellations, taken from the Shibam-Kawkaban, a minaret in the Yemen (see Figs. 6.11*a* and *b*). Clearly there are many such tilings of regular polygons. An elegant mathematical description of any such tiling is obtained by a list of the numbers of the sides of the polygons which surround any vertex of the tiling. Thus Fig. 6.11*a* is described by the code (6,4,3,4), because each point is surrounded by a hexagon (6 sides), two squares (4 sides), and a triangle (3 sides). Similarly Fig. 6.11*b*, with hexagons, dodecagons, and squares, is coded (6,12,4), and the sub-lattices of the Chinese lattice in Fig. 6.3 are coded (3,3,3,3,3,3) and (6,6,6). The Chinese lattice itself could not be described in this notation, because the tiles are not regular

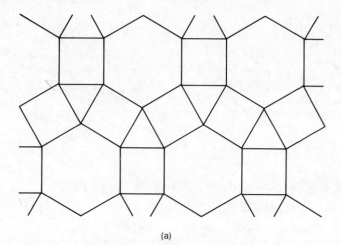

(a)

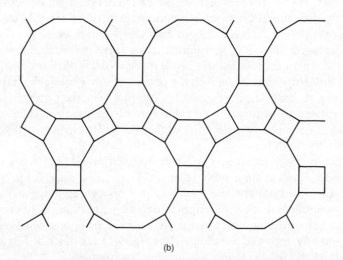

(b)

Fig. 6.11a. A tessellation of hexagons, squares, and triangles, coded (6,4,3,4), from the Shibam-Kawkaban, a minaret in the Yemen

b. A tessellation of hexagons, dodecagons, and squares, coded (6,12,4), from the Shibam-Kawkaban, a minaret in the Yemen

polygons and because the code would be different for different vertices.

This notation suggests a procedure for generating a design from a given code:

1. choose a vertex;
2. draw regular polygons round vertex with numbers of sides given in the code;
3. repeat.

But it does not predict how to find a viable code to begin with. We do not know, so far, why (6,12,4) gives a tessellation but (6,12,6) does not. The answer lies in the mathematics of regular polygons.

The angle of a polygon with n sides is calculated by the formula:

$$\text{angle} = 180 - \frac{360}{n}$$

For example, for an octagon, we have 8 sides, and the angle is

$$180 - 360 \div 8 = 135°.$$

The angles which surround any vertex must add up to 360°, so we have, for instance:

(6,12,4) gives
$$(180 - 360 \div 6) + (180 - 360 \div 12) + (180 - 360 \div 4)$$
$$= 120 + 150 + 90$$
$$= 360° \text{ so it gives a tessellation.}$$

But (6,12,6) gives $60 + 150 + 60 \neq 360°$, so it does not give a tessellation.

The mathematics now gives us a procedure or algorithm for generating tessellations: simply select combinations of angles from the following table which add up to 360°:

n	3	4	5	6	8	9	10	12
angle	60	90	108	120	135	140	144	150

This gives new designs: (4,4,4,4), (4,8,8), (3,12,12), (3,3,3,4,4), (3,3,6,6), and (3,3,4,12). Simply select the appropriate shapes and begin construction: you will find some dull and some exciting designs. For instance, the set (3,3,3,4,4) yields one dull and one attractive design. The combination (3,3,4,12) gives two different tilings, one of which is just (6,12,4) with a hexagon dissected.

The mathematics of tiling is well trodden, but has many fascinating extensions in Islamic design which seem to be less well-known or used less often. Fig. 6.12 shows a design from a thirteenth-century portal, Buyat Karatay Madrasah, from Konya in Turkey. Clearly, this figure is based on a tessellation of an irregular sixteen-sided polygon constructed from eight squares (see Fig. 6.13). Less obviously, it may be generated by a sequence of 90° rotations about its corners. This does not provide an adequate generating principle, however, because we cannot know which shapes will suffice to start with. Yet the fact that the design is based on a tessellation of squares is a clue to the solution. In Fig. 6.13 the tessellation of ABCD works by repeated rotations of 90°. A 90° rotation about D takes T_0 to T_1 and AD on to CD. Clearly, this principle only works if the line from A to D of T_0 is rotated on to the line C to D of T_1, and so of T_0. Similarly, if T_0 is to fit with T_2, then the line DC must rotate about C through 90° to obtain BC, and so on. To make a workable tile T_0, therefore, just rotate the line AD four times about successive corners of the tile.

Now we have a generating principle or algorithm for the design which surely will generalize for almost any starting line segment AD—see, for example, Fig. 6.14.

A mathematician is likely to comment that the above algorithm is far from unique. The original pattern might have been produced by many different methods, by reflections rather than rotations, for example. Fortunately, history does not tell us how the original Islamic designers invented their patterns and, consequently, we have no bias or restraint on our imagination. Any algorithm we can invent will yield new creations of our own. We transfer the principle from the square in Fig. 6.14. to a triangle in Fig. 6.15 (though the pattern breaks down if the line from A to B is not itself symmetrical!).

The beautiful design found on the Tomb Towers, Kharraqan, Iran (1459) (Fig. 6.16) can be generated in a number of ways, including the method used to produce Figs. 6.13 and 6.14. It has reflectional symmetry like Fig. 6.13 because the initial line segment is symmetrical, whereas Fig. 6.14 does not.

More and more complicated algorithms, involving either more

Fig. 6.12. A thirteenth-century portal, Buyat Karatay Madrasah, Konya, Turkey (El-Said and Parman 1976: 16, pl. 6)

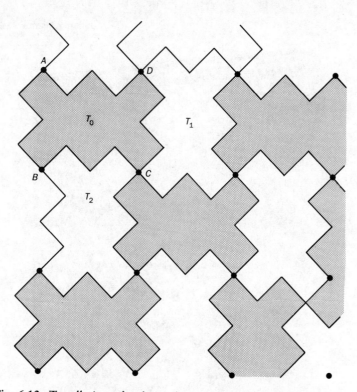

Fig. 6.13. Tessellation of a design by repeated rotations of 90°

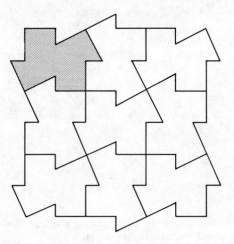

Fig. 6.14. A design constructed by the same algorithm as that used to describe Fig. 6.13

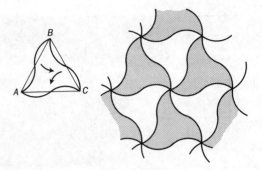

Fig. 6.15. A triangular lattice constructed by the same algorithm, with the added requirement that the line *AB* must have point symmetry about its midpoint

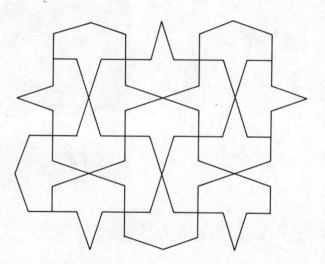

Fig. 6.16. A design found on the Tomb Tower, Kharraqan, Iran (1459) (El-Said and Parman 1976: 19, fig. 18)

complex lattices or more combinations of different transformations and symmetries, can be called into play. The process of analysis of the design, followed by synthesis into a generating algorithm or algorithms, can be very rich mathematically. The artistry lies in the ability to select from the infinity of designs, one which expresses your personal preferences.

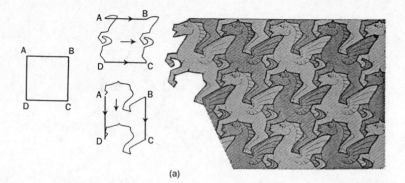

(a)

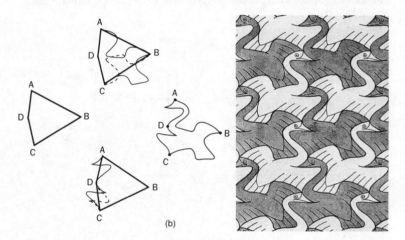

(b)

Fig. 6.17. Escher's use of translation, rotations, and reflections in generating his famous designs (Ranucci and Teeters 1977: 49, 129, 130). © M. C. Escher Foundation—Baarn—Holland. Collection Haags Gemeentemuseum, The Hague.

The graphic artist Mauritz Escher visited the Alhambra in Granada and studied its Islamic designs, spending many days copying its motifs. His interest in space-filling tessellation involved systematic application of all the crystallographic groups mentioned earlier. Figs. 6.17*a* and *b* show how he used combinations of translation, rotation, and reflection techniques to generate certain designs.

To summarize the story so far, I see the mathematical study of designs as a three-step process:

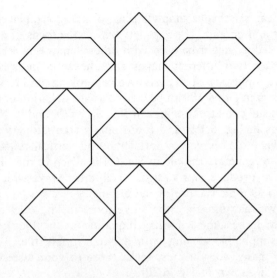

Fig. 6.18. A floor tiling from the Taj Mahal

1. describe the design geometrically;
2. devise an algorithm or algorithms for generating the design;
3. use the algorithm(s) for creating new designs and select a design to taste.

The level of geometrical description can be more or less formal, depending on the level of development of the student. For young children, the design is seen informally as a collection of shapes put together in a particular way, often with spaces left between the shapes. As the student matures and comes to understand tessellation and tiling, the design may be seen as a modification, using transformation or dissection techniques, of a regular tessellation. Finally, formal identification of the symmetries of the pattern can provide a more complete description of a design which yields a range of new patterns which are isomorphic to the original.

An important point for the teacher is that a wide range of geometrical, drawing, calculation, and transformation techniques can be applied with varying degrees of sophistication to any given design. Experience suggests, however, that the simple designs are often richest.

Consider the floor tiling of the Taj Mahal in Fig. 6.18. Young

children can see this as simply a tiling of hexagons, placed alternately flat and on end. The gaps left are not the focus of attention.
This procedure might be used with other shapes, say a rhombus,
or might use two different shapes, say a hexagon and a rhombus.
A more sophisticated analysis involves looking for a tessellation.
The pattern in Fig. 6.18 can be viewed as a tessellation of different
tiles. Consider the three tilings in Fig. 6.19a, b, and c. Note that
the tilings in Fig. 6.19a and b are purely translational, whereas
that in Fig. 6.19c involves horizontal and vertical reflections of
each cell to generate the tile in Fig. 6.19b. Each of the tilings can
be used to produce new designs in different ways which reflect
more or less the structure of the original.

Now we may use algorithms like those in Fig. 6.19 to create
designs with the same symmetrical qualities as the floor of the Taj
Mahal, simply by starting with an appropriate tile. There are
infinitely many, so you must select those to your taste, but one
variation is shown in Fig. 6.20.

The above analysis has been based mainly on informal and
formal transformation methods to generate tiling designs. But other
designs lead more naturally to different topics in geometry. An
intriguing theme in Celtic knotwork patterns is the requirement
that one should be able to draw round the entire knot without
taking the pen from the paper—i.e. that the knot is a 'traversable'
network. Fig. 6.21 reproduces George Bain's (1977) record of the
construction of these patterns.

This theme of drawing a design or pattern in one continuous
line arises in many cultures. Philip Nissen (1988) describes the
sand-drawing of the Vanuatu of Melanesia. These are networks
defined by an unbroken line finishing and starting at the same
point (see Fig. 6.22). The people traditionally accompany the
drawing with a myth, legend, or even humorous 'shaggy dog'
story. (Recurring points in the story are represented by returning
to the intersection points of the network!)

Similarly the Tchokwe people of Angola make sand-drawings
as an accompaniment to the telling of stories, proverbs, and
fables. Another African source of such networks was described
by Zaslavsky (1973): the sand-drawings of the Shongo children of
Zaïre are said to have defeated the skills of their European visitor
(see Fig. 6.23). (This time you *are* allowed to finish at a different

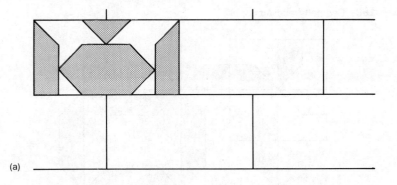

(a)

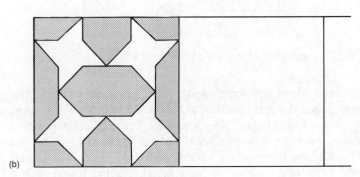

(b)

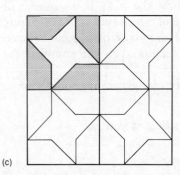

(c)

Fig. 6.19a. A tiling based on translation on a bricklayer's lattice

    b. A tiling based on a square lattice

    c. A tiling based on horizontal and vertical reflections to produce Fig. 6.19*b*

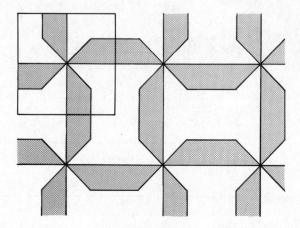

Fig. 6.20. A variation of the Taj Mahal floor tiling

point from where you start!) Apart from being fun to draw, this pattern poses the mathematical problem 'At which point(s) must you, or can you, begin?' In Figs. 6.21 and 6.22 this is not a problem, since the networks begin and end at the same point. But in Fig. 6.23 we have to find a point with 'odd' order (i.e. a point at which an odd number of lines meet). Having found such a point, is it possible to fail to draw the network?

Finally, it is amusing to try to draw the 'next' in a sequence of such drawings: or draw the middle of a sequence of three. Figure 6.24 shows a sequence of Tamil drawings of a reconstructed Brahma's knot (the symbol of protection): can you complete the sequence?

Now we can describe the algorithm for generating some Shongo networks as follows:

- start with a point and draw a line as you go
- forward 6 steps
- turn left 90°
- forward 1 step
- turn left 90°
- forward 5 steps
- turn left 90°
- forward 2 steps
- turn, etc.

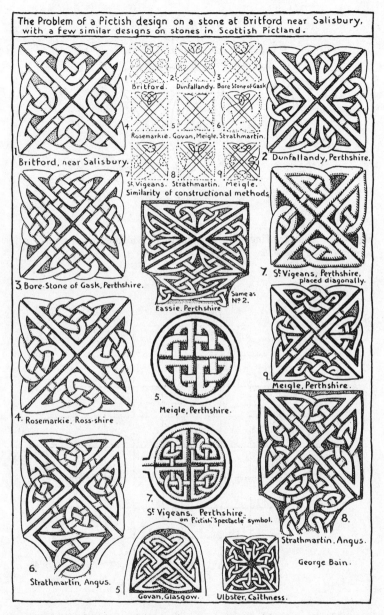

The Problem of a Pictish design on a stone at Britford near Salisbury, with a few similar designs on stones in Scottish Pictland.

1 Britford, near Salisbury. 2 Dunfallandy, Perthshire. 3 Bore-Stone of Gask, Perthshire. 4 Rosemarkie, Ross-shire. 5 Meigle, Perthshire. 6 Strathmartin, Angus. 7 St. Vigeans, Perthshire, placed diagonally. 8 Strathmartin, Angus. 9 Meigle, Perthshire.

Eassie, Perthshire. Same as No 2.

5. Meigle, Perthshire.

7. St Vigeans, Perthshire, on Pictish 'spectacle' symbol.

Govan, Glasgow. Ulbster, Caithness. George Bain.

Similarity of constructional methods.

Fig. 6.21. The Celtic method of construction of knotworks found on Scottish stones (Bain 1977: 41, pl. F)

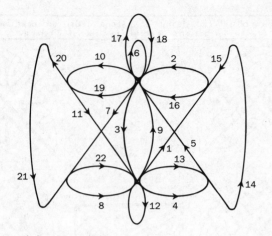

Fig. 6.22. Sand-drawing of the Vanuatu of Melanesia, formed from a continuous line (Nissen 1988: fig. 3)

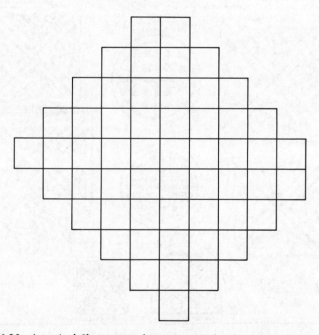

Fig. 6.23. A typical Shongo sand pattern (Zaslavsky 1973: 106)

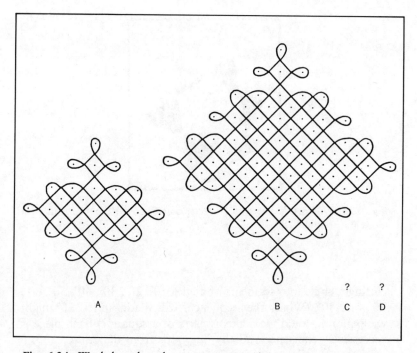

Fig. 6.24. Worksheet based on a sequence of Tamil drawings (Gerdes 1988)

The progression of numbers alternately decreases and increases:

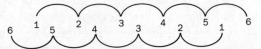

This algorithm is rapidly generalized to produce a similar network of any size. But we may consider similar networks based on any sequence. Why not, for example, the simple repetition of a Pythagorean triple, or of a sequence from the Vedic Square, or why not explore variations of the angle to be turned through?

The principle of applying geometry to art is one which is now widespread in modern art. It would be a pity if our intention of offering a multicultural context for these studies did not include examples of modern European culture.

Norman Dilworth's *Parts of a Circle* (Fig. 6.25) is created by

Fig. 6.25. Dilworth's *Parts of a Circle*, constructed from segments of a circle (Grevsmühl 1988*b*)

cutting a circle into segments of angles 10°, 20°, 30°, 40°, 50°, 60°, 70°, and 80°. (What other sequences which add up to 360° might we explore? Could we make a 'parts of a square'?) Each piece is successively translated radially outwards from the last.

In *Straight Curve* Bridget Riley draws triangles on horizontal and vertical lines with gaps which continuously change in some regular pattern. It is a simple matter to investigate how different gap widths generate different patterns. Note how the gaps between vertical lines gradually increase and then decrease again, from about 2 units to 6 units and then back again. A pupil might sketch a smooth curve for a function increasing from 2 to 6 and back to 2 again, or might be given a formula with appropriate shape to calculate the width of the nth gap.

It is a straightforward matter to explore the consequences of sketching alternative smooth curves for gap size to produce different patterns, or to explore other functions gap(n), where n is the number of the gap. A computer program will facilitate the process and allow the rapid exploration of many designs without tedium!* The key lines could be:

---

* GAPX(N) and GAPY(M) are the gapsize functions for lines parallel to the Y-axis and X-axis. PROCTRIANGLE(X,Y) is a procedure for drawing a triangle with one corner at the point with coordinates (X,Y).

Fig. 6.26. Bridget Riley's *Straight Curve*, constructed from triangles drawn on horizontal and vertical lines with appropriate gaps (Holt 1971)

```
FOR N = 1 TO ENDX
NEWY = 0
FOR M = 1 TO ENDY
NEWY = OLDY + GAPY(M)
PROCTRIANGLE(NEWX, NEWY)
NEXT M
NEWX = OLDX + GAPX(N)
NEXT N
```

In conclusion, we have shown how mathematics at every level can be abstracted from certain patterns and designs in an attempt to describe the patterns more or less formally. This can lead to the definition of an algorithm, i.e. a procedure by which the design is created from its parts. This algorithm can then lead to the creation of new designs by varying the parts of the algorithm.

By an algorithm one means only a procedure, which may be as informal as 'select hexagons and fit together' or may be formally sufficiently well defined to produce a computer program. By specifying a range of levels of procedure from very practical and simple to highly formal, we invite success for a wide range of pupils of greater or less ability and at various stages. We also invite a range of response from any one pupil, who may respond to the task spontaneously at one level, but may go on to attain a higher level response with the help of a teacher. The wide range of open-ended creative activity in response to these tasks also recommends them to teachers who are looking for problem-solving materials for geometry.

The strength of the approach of 'geometry in art' for the mathematics teacher is undoubted. The aims of education for a multicultural society are also met, to the extent that we value materials from many cultures as contexts for study. The artistic and mathematical appreciation of the products of 'other' cultures, and of 'our own', should be a valuable contribution to the positive image of many cultures which is the principal aim of multicultural or anti-racist education.

7 Statistics and Inequality: A Global Perspective

JULIAN WILLIAMS AND
GEORGE GHEVERGHESE JOSEPH

In this chapter we examine how the teaching of statistics in schools may be enriched by illustrations from the theme of economic and social inequality, a topic often seen as more appropriate for a social studies or humanities course. Inequality is an issue that dominates both individual and collective consciousness. It is the stuff of which political controversies are made. It generates a complex of human emotions from anger and helplessness to envy and guilt. At the heart of the debate lies the need for accurate statistical data and rigorous statistical interpretation, for in few areas is such a plethora of selective statistics quoted to support or discredit different positions.

The reluctance of the mathematics teacher to enter the fray is in part explained by a general disinclination to be involved in controversies. But, more importantly, there are some real doubts about the pedagogical value of examining the subject of inequality in the first place. Consider the well-known example of the banana diagram presented in Fig. 7.1. Each marked section indicates the relative share of the proceeds from its sale going to different groups involved in growing, transporting, and retailing it. The origin of this example is interesting. In a study of the export trade of Ecuador in 1975 it was found that about half of that country's export earnings came from this fruit, with the proportional distribution of the proceeds from the sale of one banana given by Fig. 7.1. There was also an investigation on how the purchasing power of bananas had changed during the previous fifteen years, relative to what could be bought with the export earnings from this crop. In

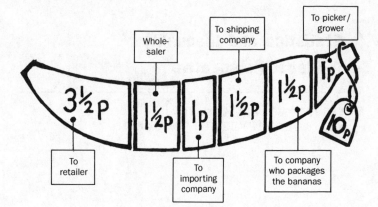

Fig. 7.1. The banana figure, as it appeared in Wilkinson (1985: 32)

1960 three tons of bananas bought one tractor. In 1975 the same tractor cost fourteen tons of bananas. An economist would say that the terms of trade of Ecuador, expressed as a ratio between the prices of one ton of bananas and one tractor, had deteriorated quite dramatically over the fifteen years.

What would be the reaction of a typical mathematics teacher to the possibility of using such information in a classroom? Would it be something along the lines: 'Presenting this information in the form given in Fig. 7.1 is close to political indoctrination. It is trying to persuade children that banana-growers are an exploited group. It is an abuse of our role in the classroom to raise issues of this sort. It is also, by the way, an example of an abuse of statistics.' When asked to elaborate on the last point, the teacher may point to the need for the areas of the sections to be in proportion to the amount represented. A banana is hardly an ideal representational form to achieve this!

The concerns of a humanities teacher tackling this topic in a classroom may well be very different. Questions relating to the production and distribution process of the banana industry need a thorough investigation before one can even start to understand the relative shares received by different groups. Are the picking and growing processes more or less labour intensive than the transportation and retailing of bananas? It is common knowledge that the preservation and storage of bananas are more capital intensive than the picking and growing processes. Also, because of the nature of the product, once brought to the retail market, it has to be sold quickly or it will rot. Before concluding that the pictogram exemplifies the exploitation of the farmers and agricultural workers of the economically underdeveloped world, a humanities teacher may well point out the necessity of comparing the lot of the banana-growers and pickers with that of, say, hop-pickers and growers in this country. Or, moving away from agriculture, the share of a computer programmer in the proceeds of commercially produced software would be another interesting example.

A common question asked of trainee mathematics teachers (or, for that matter, teachers of other disciplines as well) is: 'Are you a teacher of mathematics or a teacher of children?' The teachers of children see their primary aim as the education of the whole child, with the teaching of mathematics as subordinate to this endeavour. Where there are cross-curricular issues such as those in the example just discussed, the objective is to bring together mathematics and humanities, each providing different insights into the problem. Clearly, if statistics form an essential part of the mathematics curriculum, and if the subject of inequality is important because of its central role in economics and politics, then the statistics of inequality should be of equal concern to teachers of both mathematics and humanities.

It is all too common to see statistics being taught from examples which are not exactly inspiring.

The end-of-term marks of 100 pupils were . . .

A shop sold 20 pairs of shoes in one afternoon. Their sizes were . . .

The weights and heights of 30 children in a classroom were . . .

Technical operations involving calculations of averages or presentation of data in tables or diagrams are then performed by children, with little motivation or understanding of their relevance to life outside the classroom.

In contrast, consider the following sets of information taken from real life. Table 7.1 contains data on the causes of death of 14 million children under five years old in 1987, taken from the annual report by UNICEF entitled *The State of the World's*

Table 7.1. Deaths of children under five, developing countries, 1987

Cause of death	Number of deaths (millions)	Comments
Diarrhoeal diseases	5	A major cause of malnutrition; 3.5 million deaths caused by dehydration which could have been prevented or treated by low-cost oral rehydration therapy (ORT)
Malaria	1	Number of deaths could be drastically reduced by low-cost drugs if parents knew the symptoms and could get help
Measles	1.9	A major cause of malnutrition; can be prevented if the child is vaccinated after the age of 9 months
Acute respiratory infections	2.9	0.6 million whooping-cough deaths could be prevented by vaccinations; most of the rest could be prevented by low-cost antibiotics at the start of the infections
Tetanus	0.8	All neo-natal deaths which could be prevented by the immunization of the mother-to-be
Others	2.4	Many could be avoided by pre-natal care, breast-feeding, and nutrition education
TOTAL	14	Of about 14 million deaths, approximately 10 million are from four major causes all of which are preventable by low-cost treatment and education

Source: UNICEF (1988: 3, fig. 1).

Children (UNICEF 1988). Tables 7.2*a* and *b* contain information, taken from Hudson (1990), on the percentage of the population with access to 'safe' drinking water in two groups of countries: those with a life-expectancy rate of less than 50 years in Table 7.2*a* and those with a life-expectancy rate greater than 70 years in Table 7.2*b*.

You may be surprised to find from Table 7.1 that measles, seen as a common but hardly serious affliction in the developed world,

Table 7.2a. Access to 'safe' drinking water in countries with a life-expectancy rate of less than fifty years

Country	Life expectancy	Access to water (% of population)
Oman	49	52
Yemen, Arab Republic	43	4
Yemen, People's Democratic Republic of	46	37
Afghanistan	37	10
Bangladesh	48	68
Kampuchea	39	45
Laos	43	48
Nepal	45	11
Angola	42	17
Central African Republic	43	18
Chad	43	26
Congo	43	26
Ethiopia	46	13
Guinea	43	10
Ivory Coast	47	14
Madagascar	48	26
Malawi	44	44
Mali	45	23
Mauritania	44	17
Mozambique	49	7
Niger	45	49
Nigeria	49	28
Rwanda	46	38
Senegal	44	35
Sierra Leone	47	9
Somalia	39	38
Sudan	47	46
Togo	48	11
Uganda	48	16
Upper Volta	44	14

Source: Hudson (1990: 131–2).

still kills two million children every year. You may feel curious about Oral Rehydration Therapy (ORT) and discover how easily it can be implemented to eliminate deaths through dysentry at a stroke. You may, through constructing scatter plots such as those in Figs. 7.2*a* and *b* for the data in Tables 7.2*a* and *b* discover how close or otherwise is the association between life expectancy and accessibility to clean drinking water. A cursory examination of the diagrams indicates that the association is not very strong, though

Table 7.2b. Access to 'safe' drinking water in countries with a life-expectancy rate of more than seventy years

Country	Life expectancy	Access to water (% of population)
Canada	75	99
United States	75	99
Argentina	71	60
Costa Rica	73	81
Cuba	73	62
Jamaica	71	82
Panama	71	83
Trinidad & Tobago	72	89
Uruguay	71	78
Belgium	73	89
Denmark	75	99
France	76	97
West Germany	73	99
Greece	74	97
Italy	74	86
The Netherlands	76	97
Norway	76	98
Portugal	72	92
United Kingdom	74	99
Czechoslovakia	72	78
East Germany	73	82
Hungary	71	44
Poland	73	55
Austria	73	88
Finland	75	84
Ireland	73	73
Spain	74	78
Sweden	77	99
Switzerland	76	96
Yugoslavia	71	58
Israel	73	99
Japan	77	98
Singapore	72	100
Australia	74	97
New Zealand	74	93

Source: Hudson (1990: 131–2).

stronger for countries with a life expectancy greater than 70 years (Fig. 7.2b) than for those with a life expectancy of less than 50 years (Fig. 7.2a). Information such as this serves an important function: it involves you, makes you want to talk to others about it, and shows mathematics as both relevant and powerful.

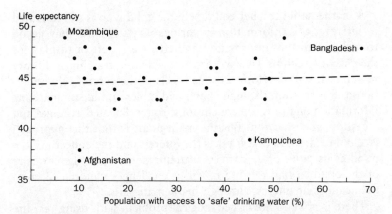

Fig. 7.2a. Scatterplot of life expectancy against percentage of population with access to 'safe' water in countries with a life-expectancy rate of less than 50 years; information for the period 1978–82 from Hudson (1990: 131–2)

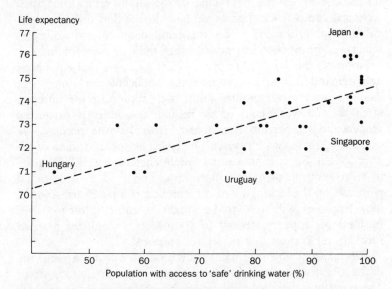

Fig. 7.2b. Scatterplot of life expectancy against percentage of population with access to 'safe' water in countries with a life-expectancy rate of more than 70 years; information for the period 1978–82 from Hudson (1990: 131–2)

A mathematics teacher could help the child who is so motivated to interpret this information in various ways. A child may go on to seek out further information and create a report or display for the class or school. This will involve valuable training in library research. It will develop statistical skills in the correct representation of information through charts and tables and in summarizing information and drawing conclusions from calculated averages and measures of dispersion. But the main point is that this approach is 'child-centred' in that it takes the interest and the concern of the pupil as its point of departure. It attempts to engage the curiosity of the child to find out more, and it challenges children to communicate their interest through mathematics.

There is a well-known pedagogical problem with using real-life data. The numbers involved often tend to be more 'awkward' than those artificially cooked for a textbook. This ceases to be a debilitating problem if children can be provided with calculators and computers to handle statistical operations. It places new emphasis on the conceptual understanding of the pupils rather than their technical competence. Just as we have learnt that providing calculators for arithmetic places the demand on student ability to select an appropriate operation rather than to perform the calculation, so the availability of statistical packages will emphasize and demand that students select the applicable technique. For example, one would require students to appreciate the different strengths and weaknesses of the median as a measure of central tendency in comparison to the mean, rather than the mechanics of calculating these two measures. Similarly, an understanding of the appropriate use of a pie chart in preference to, say, a histogram in representation of data is more important than the traditional emphasis on the techniques of construction of a pie chart. And the new emphasis will need to be taught in context, because this business of 'appropriateness' of a concept can only be grasped through application to a variety of contexts.

The major problem remains: how does one teach a child the difficult and sophisticated skill of correctly interpreting the data? The questions that may arise in relation to the two illustrations discussed earlier may include:

How many children died of diseases which would have been prevented by a comprehensive immunization programme?

Table 7.3. World grain consumption, by North and South, 1981

Area	Population (billions)	Grain consumption (people) (%)	Grain consumption (animals) (%)	Total (%)
North	1	16	46	62
South	3.3	30	8	38
TOTAL	4.3	46	54	100

Source: Hudson (1987a: 4); statistics from World Bank (1981).

By how many years could life expectancy be increased in the 'poorer' countries (i.e., those with a life expectancy of less than 50 years) if a massive world-wide programme ensured that three out of every four households (or roughly 75 per cent of the total population of those countries) had access to safe drinking water?

At one level these are mathematical questions. But there are also imponderable elements which could cause insecurity among both children and teachers who may be used to the traditional 'closed' teaching situation. For example, would a 10 per cent increase in the number of households with access to safe drinking water in Mozambique have the same impact on life expectancy as it would in Oman?

Consider another illustration, which helps to bring out the contrast between the 'open' and 'closed' approaches in teaching statistics more starkly. The data in Table 7.3 is of grain consumption by the 'North' and the 'South', as defined by the Brandt Report. An 'open' approach simply involves asking groups of children to examine this table and write down any conclusions they can draw from it. But a less 'open' approach may ask the following questions to lead the children to an understanding of the data.

1. In total, the North consumes twice as much as the South: true or false?
2. The North consumes more grain in animal production than the South does in total: true or false?
3. On average, the North uses six times more grain per person than the South: true or false?

At this point a student who has worked through the questions could be able to comment appropriately on the meaning of the data.

Table 7.4. Share of land and national income of black and white peoples of South Africa, 1981

	Population (millions)	Share of land (%)	Share of national income (%)
Black	18	13	36
White	4	87	64

Source: Hudson (1987b: 38).

Both approaches have their place with students at different levels of maturity and understanding. The 'open' approach is less likely to be judged by mathematics teachers as 'indoctrination', since the 'closed' approach must either avoid the sensitive issue of redistribution (and therefore the principal motivating issue in presenting the data in the first place) or else be found guilty of 'indoctrinating' the students to draw 'obvious' conclusions. For some teachers, a compromise is to ask 'closed' (but probably anodyne) questions and leave pupils the opportunity to raise the challenging issues for themselves.

Of course, the charge of 'indoctrination' cannot be dismissed lightly. The data in Table 7.3 is selected in such a way as to suggest redistribution between the North and South. However, it may be argued, on evidence not given here, that redistribution is not the most sensible policy in comparison to, say, one of growing more or destroying fewer crops!

Another example will serve to illustrate the same point. Table 7.4 provides information on population, share of land, and national income of people in South Africa, classified into black (i.e. those of African origin) and white (i.e. those of European origin). In an attempt to instill some 'life' into these statistics, we take twenty-two students in a class (the rest can be spectators) and divide them notionally into a black and a white population. We then calculate the approximate floor area to give to each group. For a classroom of size 8 by 5 metres, this is approximately 5m^2 and 35m^2 of space respectively for the black and the white populations. We now ask the 'black' population, eighteen of them, to squeeze into this 5m^2 and the 'white' population to spread themselves out in their assigned 35m^2. The emotions aroused by this demonstration can be intense: more telling than merely informing the class that each 'black' student has about 0.3m^2 of land compared with 8.7m^2 for the 'white'. Most students would feel that this difference is extremely unjust and oppressive.

But is this process mathematically valid? If we conduct the same experiment with twenty-two students and a football pitch, the feelings would not be so intense. And a similar demonstration, using data for Londoners and non-Londoners, may seem meaningless. The idea of assigned space per person as a measure of value is generally worthless. The validity of students' feelings of injustice, if they are valid, must rest on other statistics which are not capable of such dramatic presentation, such as the gap in the life expectancy of the two populations in South Africa or in the infant mortality rates.

The 'income' measure, on the other hand, may be valid under certain circumstances. Let 100p represent the national income, which is shared out by giving 36p to the eighteen 'blacks', while the four 'whites' receive 64p. Assuming equal shares, this would mean that each 'black' receives 2p and each 'white' 16p. But there is a serious objection to this measure, and that hinges on the concept of 'average', which is defined here to be the 'income' received by each person if the total is shared *equally*. This reminds one of the story about a child who was asked how to share sixteen lollies between eight children, and who replied that she would give them one each and keep the other eight for herself! Are equal shares a realistic assumption? We will return to this issue later.

To take stock of the arguments so far, there is a strong reason for statistics to be taught using data which are of immediate social relevance. In considering a question such as inequality, the student is shown why mathematics is both a powerful and useful tool. However, this is not to minimize the difficulties of drawing 'hard' conclusions from the applications of mathematics to complex social phenomena. There is a danger in encouraging students to draw specific conclusions based on selective data or on a limited understanding of the economics or social issues involved. It is likely that the student will draw conclusions based on their own opinions reinforced by the limited data available. But this is a reflection of all statistical work in the social sciences, albeit that the professionals are better informed. And, if students are to have a grasp of the key area of statistical interpretation, then they must experience this themselves.

The technical business of calculating and displaying statistics is useless without the ability to interpret, i.e. to make arguments from statistics and to debunk abuses of statistics. As stated earlier, the technical business is increasingly an undemanding matter. What some believe to be the division of labour between the mathematics and humanities teachers—where the former is concerned with the 'technical' aspects of statistics and the latter with the 'interpretative' aspects—is of less relevance today.

Now consider the problem that the teacher has in introducing new concepts and skills rather than in teaching students to apply those previously learnt. It would be a mistake to see the teaching of statistics in context as simply one of applying known techniques. If this were the case, then we might be happy for the humanities teacher, assuming some empathy for the mathematical development of their pupils, to deal with the whole subject.

The teacher who introduces the concept of average purely as an algorithm of calculation on a set of data, i.e.

$$(x_1, x_2 \ldots x_n) \longrightarrow \frac{(x_1 + x_2 + \ldots + x_n)}{n}$$

will fail to provide the student with the necessary conceptual framework for genuine understanding. This process can be described by the analogy of trying to follow step-by-step directions rather than using a map of the whole area. In the case of the concept of averaging, pupils should make all sorts of connections, such as:

- the average is what each gets when the goods are shared equally;
- the average is between the largest and the smallest value, roughly in the middle;
- it is highly unlikely that the average is a description of anything that exists in real life (an average family has been described as an overworked wife, an underpaid husband, and 2.2 children);
- everyone would get the average if those above the average gave some to those below the average;
- there are different types of averages and different ways of calculating them: compare cricket averages with golf averages or compare the three common average measures in statistics, i.e. mean, median, and mode.

Table 7.5. Calculation of weighted average income of black and white peoples of South Africa, based on Table 7.4

	People		Average share (pence)		Total (pence)
Black	18	×	2	=	36
White	4	×	16	=	64
TOTAL	22	×	?	=	100

These connections will be achieved and a sound basis for understanding attained only if the students explore the concept as it is experienced in real-life situations. 'The 2p per black person' in South Africa was a case in point. This was not an *application* of the algorithm of calculating a measure but a preliminary exercise to introduce the concept.

The notion of equal shares and, hence, of redistribution is one which is fundamental to the concept of average. The redistribution of income in the South African example played out by twenty-two students yields an overall average of about 5p per student. If each of the 'whites' with 16p retains 5p and the remaining 11p are redistributed among the 'blacks', this provides an effective representation of the concept of averaging. We have also, in the process of calculating the overall average, introduced the new idea of a frequency distribution and the method of calculating 'weighted' averages:

$$\text{average (or } \bar{x} \text{)} = \frac{\Sigma f x}{\Sigma f} = \frac{f_1 x_1 + f_2 x_2 + \ldots}{f_1 + f_2 + \ldots}$$

where the number of people represents the frequency (f) and the share received by each person is the variate x. In our example, the average share is:

$$\bar{x} = \frac{(18 \times 2 + 4 \times 16)}{18 + 4} = \frac{100}{22} = \text{approx. 5p.}$$

The next example illustrates another aspect of the averaging and redistribution process. The bar chart on the left of Fig. 7.3 shows the calorie consumption per person in each of four countries, expressed as a percentage of the basic calorie requirements per person. The information contains no surprises. Overconsump-

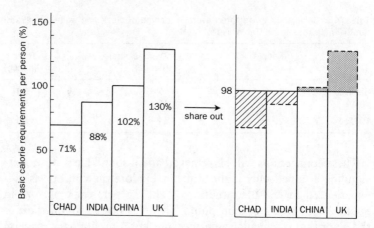

Fig. 7.3. Calorie consumption per person expressed as a percentage of the basic calorie requirements per person, for four countries, and the effect of a simple sharing out, 1981 (Hudson 1987a: 4)

tion in the United Kingdom has its reverse in the calorie deficiencies in India and Chad. China, at just over 100 per cent, represents the example of a country where the average supply meets average needs. An interesting question is: suppose we redistributed calorie consumption of the four countries mentioned above equally, could we meet the basic needs of all people in these countries?

It is tempting to try to redistribute the columns in the manner shown on the right of Fig. 7.3. This implies a simple average of the form:

$$\bar{x} = \frac{x_1 + x_2 + x_3 + x_4}{4}$$

But a moment's reflection will show that this is a meaningless average. Even if the columns represented the total calories consumed by each country, this would be a most unfair redistribution because it takes no account of differences in the population size of the four countries. A more suitable average would be:

$$\bar{x} = \frac{f_1 x_1 + f_2 x_2 + f_3 x_3 + f_4 x_4}{f_1 + f_2 + f_3 + f_4} = \frac{\text{total calories}}{\text{total population}}$$

Table 7.6. Distribution of household income, Honduras and United Kingdom, 1981

Countries	Percentage share of total household income					
	Lowest 20%	Second 20%	Third 20%	Fourth 20%	Top 20%	Total (100%)
Honduras	2.3	5.0	8.0	16.9	67.8	100
United Kingdom	7.4	11.7	17.0	24.7	39.2	100

Source: Hudson (1987a: 9).

This example provides a natural and motivating context in which to introduce the averaging of a frequency distribution as a form of 'equal distribution' among populations.

Many readers will recognize that, in fact, the problem of inequality is found as much *within* countries as *between* countries. To illustrate, consider the household income distribution in two countries, Honduras and the United Kingdom. The information may be presented in the form of a table (see Table 7.6) or by means of diagrams (see Fig. 7.4a and b). The households are divided into five equal groups, according to the size of their incomes. Thus, as can be seen from Table 7.6 and Fig 7.4a, the top 20 per cent of UK households receive 39.2 per cent of the total UK income. Table 7.6 allows limited mainly pairwise comparisons between income groups, as shown in Fig. 7.4a. To obtain an overall picture of differences in the distribution of incomes, a cumulative diagram, such as Fig. 7.4b, is more revealing. This is based on the percentage of total household income received by the lowest 20, 40, 60, 80 per cent of households. So, for example, the lowest 40 per cent of household incomes in Honduras account for 2.3 + 5.0 = 7.3 per cent of total household income.

A question immediately arises: of the two countries, which one has a more equitable distribution of income? A glance at Fig. 7.4b would be sufficient to answer the question: in the United Kingdom, 60 per cent of the population receives about 36 per cent of the total income while in Honduras the same percentage of the population receives only 15 per cent of the total income. However, there are two questions whose answers are not readily obvious from Fig. 7.4b.

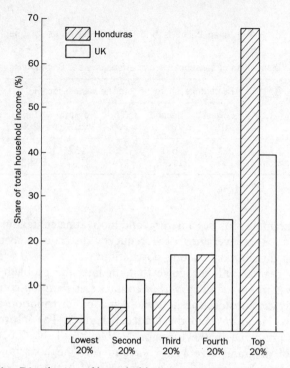

Fig. 7.4a. Distribution of household income, Honduras and United Kingdom: a comparative bar chart

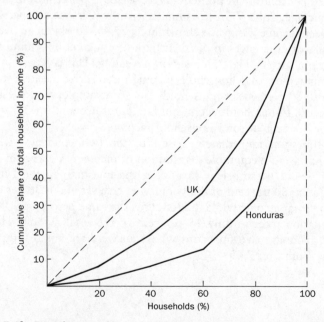

Fig. 7.4b. Distribution of household income, Honduras and United Kingdom: a cumulative diagram

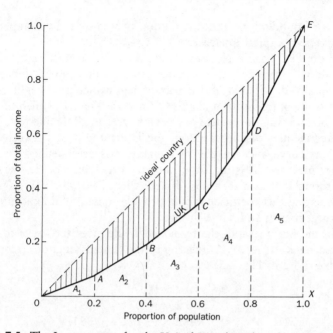

Fig. 7.5. The Lorenz curve for the United Kingdom, based on Table 7.6 (the shaded area is half the Gini coefficient) (Hudson 1987*a*: 9)

If we were comparing more than two countries, is there a single measure of inequality which will help us to rank these countries?

If we are examining the trends in income distribution in one or more country, is there some summary indicator that we could use?

The representation given in Fig. 7.5 would provide answers to both questions. In 1905 Lorenz suggested a method of measuring the concentration of wealth in a given population. In a graphical presentation, Lorenz represented on the *x*-axis the cumulated proportion of the population from the poorest to the richest and on the *y*-axis the cumulated proportion of the total wealth held by that population. The Lorenz curve, constructed on the basis that its upper and lower extremities are (1,1) and (0,0) respectively, has a number of economic and social applications, including, apart from distributions of income or wealth, geographical concentrations of populations and distribution of industries by number of workers or capital intensity.

From Fig. 7.5 it is clear that any Lorenz curve must lie between the dotted line which indicates the 'ideal' country in which income is equally distributed and a pair of perpendicular straight lines consisting of the horizontal axis OX and the line XE, which shows the bizarre situation where one person receives all the income. The more unequal the distribution, the larger the area between the Lorenz curve and the line of equality; this area defines a summary measure. This measure, known as the Gini coefficient, can be thought of as a measure of inequality. Two different ways of calculating this coefficient could provide some useful exposure to both geometry and curve-fitting.

In the first method, the trapezoidal rule gives the areas of the trapeziums A_1, A_2 ... A_5 relating to the United Kingdom (refer to Table 7.6 and Fig. 7.5) as:

$$A_1 = 0.5 \times 0.2 \times 0.074$$
$$A_2 = 0.5 \times 0.2 \times (0.074 + 0.191)$$
$$A_3 = 0.5 \times 0.2 \times (0.191 + 0.361)$$
$$A_4 = 0.5 \times 0.2 \times (0.361 + 0.608)$$
$$A_5 = 0.5 \times 0.2 \times (0.608 + 1.000)$$

Total = $0.5 \times 0.2 [2(0.074 + 0.191 + 0.361 + 0.608) + 1.000]$
= 0.3394

Therefore, the shaded area in Fig. 7.5 is estimated to be

$$0.5 - 0.3394 = 0.1606.$$

Doubling this result would give the Gini coefficient as 32 per cent. The reader may wish to check that following the same steps of calculation would give the Gini coefficient for Honduras as 58 per cent. This coefficient is a measure of inequality on the scale 0 per cent to 100 per cent, where the two extreme values represent the situation of perfect equality and inequality respectively. It is now possible to rank countries on this scale, with Honduras showing greater inequality in the distribution of income compared to the United Kingdom.

Empirical work in economics has found that estimates of the Gini coefficient worked out by this method have a downward

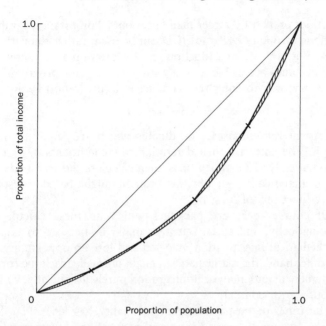

Fig. 7.6. The error (shaded area) in the trapezoidal estimate of the area under the Lorenz curve

bias. In other words, the real coefficient is greater than the trapezoidal estimate. The reason for this is not hard to see. The Lorenz curve in Fig. 7.5 is smooth. The trapezoidal estimate uses straight lines OA, AB, BC, CD, and DE to approximate to the curve and calculates the area of the polygon $OABCDEX$. The real coefficient would be calculated using the area under the curve $OABCDE$, which is clearly less than the area of the polygon. The shaded area is therefore clearly more than the estimate obtained from the trapezoidal rule.

The trapezoidal estimate can be improved in two ways. The most obvious way is to increase the number of trapeziums involved in the estimate until the error (shaded heavily in Fig. 7.6) becomes small enough to be ignored. In the limit as the number of trapeziums is increased, the 'definite integral' of the function is obtained, a fundamental concept in sixth-form calculus.

Alternatively, the curve can be approximated using quadratic functions of 'best fit' rather than linear ones. For instance, parabolic sections through OAB and BCD can be used, rather than straight lines. With the aid of a function graph plotter on a computer, this task becomes accessible to many students. In some programs, it is necessary only to enter the data, select a quadratic function,

$$y = ax^2 + bx + c,$$

and point the cursor at coordinates which are required on the graph. The software then determines the coefficients a, b, and c automatically. The student may then calculate the area under the curve analytically. An obvious thought might be to investigate other functions of 'best fit'.

Of course there are packages which do these calculations automatically, and social scientists might be inclined to skip the mathematical investigation involved and lose an opportunity. On the other hand, the mathematician might normally teach the concept of numerical and analytical integration purely graphically, without recourse to a context.

The topic of measurement of inequality has led us far from simple average to curve-fitting and integration. Apart from providing an introduction to concepts in descriptive statistics such as cumulative frequency graphs, mean and median, and curve-fitting, it helps to develop the skills of looking at statistical measures critically. It also allows interpretation to take place immediately. There is no 'two-year time delay' between learning a technique in the abstract and being capable of applying it meaningfully to a good problem.

Some of the more difficult concepts in statistics relate to inference from samples. We now examine how such concepts can be made more accessible through providing appropriate contexts. Consider the following question:

Why are there so few black* MPs in the House of Commons? (4 out of 630 in 1991)

Intuitively one would expect, all things being equal, that the number of black MPs would reflect the proportion of blacks in the

---

* The word *black* is here used to describe minority populations in the United Kingdom, predominantly of Asian and West Indian origin.

Table 7.7. The number of black MPs in 30 and 100 000 simulated parliaments

30 parliaments		100 000 parliaments	
Number of black MPs	Number of parliaments	Number of black MPs	Number of parliaments
21–25	2	1–20	1528
26–30	7	21–30	39 349
31–35	11	31–40	52 966
36–40	7	41–50	6066
41–45	3	51–60	91
TOTAL	30	TOTAL	100,000

population, i.e. 5 per cent of 630 or thirty-two black MPs. But is four 'about thirty-two', or is it significantly less? After all, if you toss a coin ten times, you do not always get five heads. Let us suppose that the chance of each MP being black is one-twentieth, the same proportion as for the population as a whole. This supposition is called a 'null hypothesis'. Then assume the 630 MPs are a random selection of the population as a whole. Now let us build a model of a general election, using a sample bottle containing nineteen white beads and one black bead. The bottle is shaken and turned upside down, showing either a white or black bead in a viewing hole. We presume that each bead has an equal chance of falling into the viewing hole, so that the probability of a black bead showing is one in twenty. Let this represent the election of a black MP.

If this experiment is repeated by a child 630 times by hand or simulated on a calculator (or a computer), what results is a model of a 'parliament'. Table 7.7 gives the number of black MPs in 30 and 100 000 simulated parliaments. (Note that not one parliament elected as few as four black MPs.)

Most students appreciate that random number generation to model the election of MPs can be achieved using a calculator or computer.* With this tool, we can rapidly elect thousands of

---

* The key lines in BASIC are:

```
FOR K = 1 TO 630
IF RND(1) < 0.05 THEN B = B + 1
NEXT K
```

parliaments and record the distribution of the number of black MPs. More advanced statistical theory shows that this distribution approximates to a normal distribution, with an average of one-twentieth of 630 (or about thirty-two MPs), with 99 per cent of the distribution concentrated in the range 32 ± 14, i.e. 18–46 MPs. In fact, the theory indicates a parliament with only four black MPs or less will occur less than one in a hundred thousand times in this model. The mathematics is telling us that the model wrongly represents reality!

The idea of a mathematical model needs some thought here. It is a crucial concept in statistics, even at an elementary level. And yet it receives little mention in pre-16 syllabuses, or in the National Curriculum. Let us examine the idea of a 'model' of a general election. The ideal is that we represent a real election by a simplified process which is amenable to statistical analysis. Each parliament consists of 630 elections, with each election being a poll for a number of candidates who have been selected by their parties. So much for the reality.

In the model, each election is represented by a two-outcome sample space (black, white), with probabilities 1/20, 19/20 respectively. The parliament consists of 630 repeated samples, where each sample is independent of the other. From the model, a probabilistic prediction would give thirty-two black candidates; and we can be 95 per cent confident that there will be between twenty-three and forty-two candidates—the probabilistic inference being based on the normal distribution. However, our expected figures are contradicted by reality, and in that sense the model is a poor predictor of reality. So we need to re-examine the assumption on which the model was based. If we can introduce some modification to the assumption, we may arrive at a 'better' model, which predicts the reality more accurately.

To express this in terms of the language of hypothesis testing, we would say that the null hypothesis was our assumption that the parliament was a random sample of the population as a whole, at least as far as the ethnic composition was concerned. This hypothesis has been proved false at least 95 out of a 100 times. Consequently, the null hypothesis must be rejected (or the alternative hypothesis must be accepted). The parliament is not a random sample of the population.

Why, then, does this bias exist? An immediate suspicion is that selection of candidates and election procedures are racist, in that they strongly favour white candidates because of their race. However, there are a number of other factors which we might examine—the crucial point being that the statistical test has proved only that the parliament is not a randomly chosen sample of the population. The test cannot locate the lack of randomness in the election procedure.

Many factors might be taken into account other than race in explaining the situation. When, for example, statistics show that the IQ of black children is, on average, significantly lower than that of white children in the United States, it would be foolish to draw the conclusion that the difference in IQ is 'explained' by race. Rather, we should be asking questions about possible bias in the IQ testing procedure, as well as differences in socio-economic conditions of the two groups. In fact, when these and other factors are taken into account, a statistician concludes that 'we should rightly question the good sense or goodwill of anyone who claimed' that race was a significant causal factor (Swann Report 1985: Annex D, ch. 3, p. 148).

Can a statistician help in understanding how such variables can be taken into account? The example of black MPs is a good one for illustrating the process. One can examine the socio-economic backgrounds of current MPs and observe that they are by no means 'typical' of the population at large. There are forty-one women MPs (in 1991), which makes them 6 per cent of the total members, whereas there are just over 50 per cent of women in the electorate. There are no MPs under the age of twenty-five. Most MPs come from a privileged educational background, and many are recruited from middle-class occupations in business and the professions.

Consider, first, age. On the whole, the black population is younger than the white, mainly because it is the product of immigration in the last three decades and therefore consists predominantly of young men and women with small children. We observe that, in the selection of candidates and MPs, men of middle age are generally preferred, and so we would expect to see disproportionately more whites than blacks in the House of Commons. The question is, though, would this difference be enough to account for the small number of black MPs in parliament?

Only a further statistical analysis would reveal the answer. But

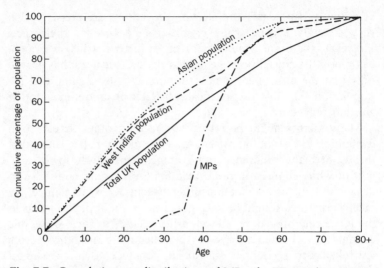

Fig. 7.7. Cumulative age distributions of MPs, the West Indian population, the Asian population, and the total UK population (Brown (1984: 30) for 1982; Mellors (1978: 29–31) for 1974–9)

an 'educated' guess can be made from looking at Fig. 7.7, which shows the cumulative age distribution of four groups in 1981: (1) MPs, (2) population of West Indian origin, (3) population of Asian origin, and (4) total population. The median ages of the four groups can be read off from the graph as 41 years for the MPs, 24 years for the West Indians, 23 years for the Asians, and 33 years for the total population. Also from the diagram, it may be observed that 50 per cent of the MPs are aged between 37 and 48 years, these being roughly the lower and upper quartiles of the distribution. The corresponding lower and upper quartiles of the age distribution of the populations of West Indians, Asians, and the total are 12 and 44 years, 12 and 38 years, and 19 and 50 years respectively. It is clear that, compared to the other three population groups, the spread of MPs' ages is over a narrower and higher band. The MPs are a more homogeneous group than the total population. Any meaningful statistical comparison should now take account of differences in the age-structures of the four groups.

To take account of the age factor, we may apply a 'stand-

Table 7.8. Socio-economic profile of different groups in the United Kingdom

Group	Professional and business	Others
West Indian origin	7	93
Asian origin	14	86
White	22	78
Conservative MPs	100	–
Labour MPs	73	27

Sources: Brown (1984: 223) for 1982; Mellors (1978: 61) for 1974–9.

ardization' procedure which involves calculating the expected number of black MPs if the black population has the same age structure as the total population. The difference between the expected and actual number of black MPs would provide a measure of the effect of differences in the age structure of two groups on the relative number of black MPs. Such a calculation (not shown here) would show that age is a minor factor in explaining the relatively small numbers of black MPs. Can we think of more significant factors which not only separate the MPs from the general population but also explain the black–white differentials?

Table 7.8 shows the socio-economic profiles for various groups within the United Kingdom. It reveals a very atypical distribution of socio-economic backgrounds among MPs. But while important differences are discernible between Labour and Conservative MPs, our focus of interest is on socio-economic differences between different groups.

The question can now be restated: if we take account of the predominantly middle-class background of MPs and the predominantly working-class occupations of the black community, does this account for the bias in parliament against black MPs? We can build a model which takes account of occupational background and, ignoring age, sex, and any other factors, predicts the distribution of black MPs in a 'model parliament', as before.

This time we need two different sampling bottles representing professional and business classes (cuboid beads) and working classes (spherical beads).*

* Roughly, the 'professional and business classes' consist of the socio-economic class groups I and II while the 'working classes' are the other socio-economic groups III–V.

The number of black and white cuboids will represent the proportion of black and white people of professional and business class, say about 0.3 and 12.5 million respectively. So let us put two black and ninety-eight white cuboids in this bottle. Similarly, we calculate that, in the 'working-class' bottle, there should be six black and ninety-four white spherical beads. Remember these represent the proportion of black and white people of the middle class (cuboids) and working class (spheres).

Now we model a simplified parliament by electing 350 Conservative MPs and 250 Labour MPs, presuming a parliament of 600 MPs and ignoring other parties. That is, we shake the middle-class bottle 350 times for Conservative and 182 times (i.e. 73 per cent of 250) for Labour. Then we shake the working-class bottle 68 times (i.e. 27 per cent of 250) for Labour, and so elect a 'parliament'.

A-level students could now calculate the expected number of black MPs to be 15 (8 Labour and 7 Conservative) and the proportion of model parliaments in which only four black MPs or less are elected is still very small. Lower down the school, random number generation will simulate the process and lead to the same conclusion, that is:

- a model which takes account of socio-economic class is a better model, more nearly fitting reality;
- the model is still inadequate, and other factors need to be accounted for.

This process of model validation, i.e. comparing the model predictions with reality, is an important part of any worthwhile statistics course. A failure to deal with it, in an appropriate form, must lead to students lacking a basic understanding of the nature and role of probability and statistics. The strength of the above examples lies in the method of reaching conclusions. What began as hunches, has led inexorably to conclusions which have mathematical validity. It shows the importance of the power of rational argument over the expression of personal opinion. The mathematical approach does seem to emphasize the exercise of the mind over emotions—particularly important in subjects which have strong emotive content. There is a further benefit in a mathematics classroom of applying statistics to a social problem of contemporary interest. The context also helps to reinforce a student's understanding of certain key concepts in statistics. The concept of median age and interquartile range as measures of central tendency and dispersion are understood in the context as indices of the peculiarity of the MPs as a social group. The cumulative frequency diagram contrasts the age distribution of the black population with that of the general population. The key idea of testing a null hypothesis is concretized in the context of addressing an important social problem: is the selection and election of black MPs biased?

Let us look at a new context in which the statistics can enter the classroom: an investigation of the nature and strength of relationships (or associations) between two or more variables. The subject of inequality provides some interesting examples. Consider an earlier example, the relationship between life expectancy and the availability of clean water based on the information given in Tables 7.2a and b. Often, the inference is made that there is a strong direct causal link between availability of clean water (cause) and long life (effect). Statistics provides a means of testing the strength of such an association. Two measures of correlation are directly derived from the information. From the data given in Tables 7.2a and b, the product moment correlation coefficient (i.e. Pearson correlation coefficient) gives coefficient values of +0.06 and +0.60 for the group of countries with a life expectancy of less than 50 and the group with a life expectancy greater than 70.

To understand the meaning of these calculated values, let us return to the scatterplots shown on Figs. 7.2a and b. The scatter of points would provide a good indication of whether the relationship between the two variables (i.e. life expectancy and access to 'safe' drinking water) is *linear* in form (i.e. whether a straight line summarizes the relationship adequately). The adequacy of such a summarization (i.e. how good a fit is to a straight line) of inexact relationships is partly a function of the *extent of scatter* of the points around an imaginary straight line (see Figs. 7.2a and b) and partly on whether the pattern of points shows *linearity* and not *curves*. It is in cases where such a linear pattern is assumed to be present that measures have been devised to examine the strength of relationship. One of the most widely used measures is the Pearson product moment correlation coefficient (usually denoted as r). It

can be demonstrated that, if the two variables are *perfectly* cor-
related, then r will have a value of either +1 or −1. In case of
imperfect correlation −1 < r < 1. If r = 0, this means that there is
no *linear* relationship between the two variables. In our example
the correlation coefficient value of 0.06 in the case of the first
group of countries with life expectancy of less than 50 years indicates that there is *no* linear relationship between the two variables, while a value of 0.60 for the second group of countries with
a life expectancy greater than 70 years indicates the existence of
some positive correlation between the two variables. However, the
existence of a positive correlation is no indication of a *causal* link
between life expectancy and access to a 'safe' water supply.

To calculate the second correlation measure, students are asked
to rank the countries, separately for the two sets of data, in an
ascending order according to their life expectancies and access to
safe drinking water, and then to consider the degree of agreement
between the two sets of ranks as shown by the rank correlation
coefficient (i.e. Spearman correlation coefficient). The rank correlation coefficients relating to the first group of countries (those
with a life expectancy of less than 50 years) is +0.05 and for the
second group (those with a life expectancy greater than 70 years)
is +0.52.

The nature of the association indicated by these statistics would
serve as a useful focus for a wide-ranging discussion on:

1. the interpretation of these statistics, including why there is
   a greater difference in the Pearson correlation coefficients
   compared to the Spearman correlation coefficients for the
   two sets of data;
2. the validity of the Spearman correlation coefficient as a
   measure of association for data where there are a number of
   'tied ranks' present;
3. the differences between statistical modelling and causal modelling;
4. the problems of making inferences with such statistics calculated from variables at different levels of measurement; and
5. the linking up of regression and correlation analysis.

The issues raised by 1–4 will not be discussed here. However,
linking up regression and correlation analysis is an exercise which

offers salutary lessons for a senior class. The 'line of best fit' for the two sets of data can be expressed in terms of the following equations:

life expectancy under 50 years
$$Y = 44.483 + 0.012X$$

life expectancy over 70 years
$$Y = 67.276 + 0.073X$$

where Y = expectation of life at birth and X = percentage of population having access to 'safe' drinking water (see Figs. 7.2a and b).

There are a range of skills tested through this example. Apart from the technical issues, relating to the validity of the assumptions behind such a procedure (such as those of linearity, uncorrelated disturbances, and non-stochastic 'explanatory' variables) and the interpretation of the regression coefficients, there are broader questions as to why the first equation offers a poorer 'fit' (as measured by the squared Pearson correlation coefficient) than the second to their respective sample data. There is more variability in the data relating to those countries with a life expectancy of less than 50 years, with certain 'outliers' such as Afghanistan, Guinea, Mozambique, and Sierra Leone—to take four countries recording households with 'safe' water supply as low as 10 per cent or less. Would the omission of these countries improve the 'goodness of fit' of the estimated equation. What determined the choice of the countries included in the sample? These and other issues provide some scope for interesting discussion in an A-level statistics class.

To conclude, we have seen how the subject of statistics at every level can be taught in a social context: the study of inequality. This brings together two important areas from the mathematics and humanities curriculum. What are the benefits to the curriculum of teaching these two subjects together?

For the mathematics teacher, the benefits are threefold. First, the topic itself may be exciting and motivating; such statistics can be dramatic and inferences challenging. Secondly, mathematics is seen to be useful, it sheds light on important issues. Thirdly, many statistical concepts can be best understood in such a context; for example, the concept of average makes most sense in the context of redistribution.

For the humanities teacher, the topic is itself important; the motivational factor is relevant too. But why join forces with the mathematics teacher? The strongest reason here is important to any teacher concerned with anti-racist multicultural education. The important aim must be to encourage children and students to treat issues of race, gender, and inequality rationally. The use of data and mathematical analysis tends to encourage objectivity and makes arguments less prone to emotive, irrational, and prejudiced attitudes. When discussing racism, all views are not equal; those which are supported by reasoned, statistical, and mathematical arguments are more equal than those which are not.

8 Envoi

The preceding chapters propose that the incorporation of a multicultural or global element in the teaching of mathematics is both feasible and advantageous. We have tried to support this with general arguments, a collection of examples in key areas of the curriculum, and detailed discussion of four contrasting topics. Like all efforts to improve education, it represents a beginning and not an end. However, at this stage we believe we have provided sufficient ideas and materials for a period of development in the classroom to follow. We hope the volume will assist the preliminary or in-service training of teachers who feel they are not at present confident or knowledgeable enough to adopt the approach.

This seems the appropriate place to reflect on the selection of material for the book.

1. On a number of occasions we found ourselves advocating materials for inclusion not primarily for mathematical reasons but because they offered valuable contributions to social, cultural, or artistic education. The topic of calendars is a case in point.

2. By contrast, some of the cultural materials were included principally to assist mathematics teaching—helping to strengthen concepts, improve motivation, or encourage investigation. Sometimes we were slow to realize the potential value of these materials. The sections in Chapter 3 on square and cube roots and on non-European board games are good examples of such situations.

3. As teachers we kept reminding ourselves of the possible mismatch between the child's culture and that of the school. The teacher, enthusing about the geometric richness of Botswana

basketwork, must not be blind to the same richness in the logos and hubcaps of the cars in the nearest car-park. This calls for a sharing of ideas and interests in the classroom—the maintenance of what we have called the 'conversation'.

4. The need to use the multicultural approach selectively and judiciously was underlined by the amount of material we rejected. This included statistics that oversimplified complex issues, materials in which the cultural element was of no more than token value, and topics such as indeterminate equations.

5. We tried to strike a balance between two types of material—the *historical* and the *contemporary*.

The former has a number of attractive features. It shows mathematics to be a global activity to which distinctive and similar contributions have been made in widely separated locations. Regardless of race or creed, humans have pursued mathematics and this pursuit is a *noncontroversial* vehicle for multicultural education. But we have become increasingly aware of the demands the historical approach makes on teachers. It is clear that, for it to be effective, support materials will be needed and a systematic input of history into the education of mathematics teachers will be needed.

On the face of it, the contemporary approach seems more straightforward. However, as our statistical examples show, the teacher must be prepared to work on controversial ground. There is scope here for the 'informed opportunist' who is well prepared and adroit enough to extract mathematical advantage from current affairs and daily life.

In conclusion we believe that the multicultural approach is important and valuable but that, like other innovations—practical mathematics, use of computers, mathematical investigations—it needs confident and flexible teachers to implement it. The task is to encourage and prepare teachers for this important and rewarding mission.

Bibliography

AL-KHWARIZMI, *Algebra*: *see* Mohammed ben Musa.

ASCHER, M., AND ASCHER, R. (1980), *Code of the Quipu* (Chicago: University of Michigan Press).

(The quipu, a versatile Inca counting and recording device made out of knotted strings, is analysed both for its cultural and historical dimensions and for its mathematical relevance. The book has useful examples for classroom investigations.)

BAIN, G. (1977), *Celtic Art: The Methods of Construction* (London: Constable).

(A book containing many examples of the Celtic art of knotwork, key patterns, and lettering. There is detailed information on their method of construction and it includes many plates of stones, shields, and embroidery. A useful library reference.)

BALL, J. (1989), *Games from around the World* (Wetherby: MBA Publishing).

(Simple enthusiastic introductions to over thirty games, from all parts of the globe. Some are very simple and most are of great antiquity. They can all be played on home-made boards using beans or coins. A valuable resource book for both the junior and the senior classroom.)

BALL, W. W. ROUSE (1892), *Mathematical Recreations and Problems* (London: Macmillan).

—— and COXETER, H. S. M. (1939), *Mathematical Recreations and Essays* (London: Macmillan).

(A classic, revised repeatedly and lately by H. S. M. Coxeter, it contains an informative chapter on magic squares.)

BELL, R. C., and CORNELIUS, M. (1988), *Board Games around the World* (Cambridge: Cambridge University Press).

(The book describes sixty games from many countries grouped as games of position, 'mancala' games, war games, race games, dice, calculator, and other games. It contains advice to teachers on using the book and suggests mathematical investigations for the classroom. Answers supplied for earlier questions. A good bibliography.)

BISHOP, A. (1988), *Mathematical Enculturation: A Cultural Perspective on Mathematics Education* (Dordrecht: Kluwer Academic).

(A stimulating book which views mathematical knowledge as a social and cultural product.)

BISHOP, A. (1990), 'Western Mathematics: The Secret Weapon of Cultural Imperialism', *Race and Class*, 32 (2), 51–65.

(A powerfully argued case for recognizing the dangers implicit in the westernized and Europeanized version of mathematics which pervades all mathematics classrooms.)

BOGOSHI, J., NAIDOO, K., and WEBB, J. (1987), 'The Oldest Mathematical Artefact', *Mathematical Gazette*, 458: 294.

(A note containing a photograph and details of a baboon fibula with twenty-nine notches found in Border Cave in the Lebombo Mountains of Southern Africa.)

BOURGOIN, J. (1973), *Arabic Geometrical Pattern and Design* (New York: Dover).

(A collection of 190 plates of traditional Islamic patterns and designs, photo-copiable but without sources. In addition, each plate provides some guidance on the construction of the pattern. A very useful teaching resource.)

BOYER, C. B. (1974), *A History of Mathematics* (New York: Wiley).

(A widely known and reliable history of mathematics whose coverage of non-European mathematics, and particularly Chinese mathematics, is more detailed and less condescending than many other similar texts.)

BRANDT REPORT (1980), *North–South—A Programme for Survival* (London: Pan Books).

(A report by an independent commission on international development issues under the chairmanship of Willy Brandt which highlighted the inequitable nature of economic relationships between the developed and underdeveloped worlds.)

BROWN, C. (1984), *Black and White Britain: The Third PSI Survey* (Aldershot: Heinemann).

(A full and detailed analysis of the third PSI survey, gathered in 1982, which contains statistics and analysis of ethnic origins, household structure and housing, language and education, employment, racial attacks, and attitudes.)

BUNYARD, D., and BRINE, A. (1988), 'Islamic Art: Vedic Square', *Micromaths*, 4 (1), 10–11.

(A short article on the use of the Vedic square to generate patterns on a computer.)

CAJORI, F. (1893), *A History of Mathematics* (New York: Macmillan).

(A book worth consulting even today for its detailed and relatively unbiased account of non-European mathematics, especially Arab and Indian mathematics.)

CALLINGER, R. (1982) (ed.), *Classics of Mathematics* (Illinois: Moore Publishing Company).

(A source book of original texts or commentaries from early times to 1932. There is some material on Babylonian, Egyptian, Mayan, Indian, and Arab mathematics.)

CARBY, H. (1980), 'Multi-culture', *Screen Education*, 34: 62–70.

(One of the early criticisms of multicultural education.)

CENTRAL STATISTICAL OFFICE (1986), *Key Data 1986* (London: HMSO).

(A selection of statistics intended for general readership. One of the sources used in our discussion of the British population in the 'Percentage' section of Chapter 3.)

CLOSS, M. P. (1986) (ed.), *Native American Mathematics* (Austin, Tex.: University of Texas Press).
(A collection of thirteen essays on the development of mathematics in various native American groups, such as the Nootka, Aztecs, Maya, Incas, and Amazon Indians. Topics discussed include number systems, number representation, geometry, and calendrical systems.)

COARD, B. (1971), *How the West Indian Child is made Educationally Subnormal in the British School System* (London: New Beacon Books).
(An influential book which highlights the general underachievement of West Indian children and examines the causes, including the way teachers handle black children, their low expectations of the children, and their readiness to label them as trouble-makers.)

COCKCROFT REPORT: *see* Department of Education and Science (1982).

COLE, M., GAY, J., GLICK, J. A. and SHARP, D. W. (1971), *The Cultural Context of Learning and Thinking* (London: Methuen).
(A major study of the logic, language, and performance in cognitive tasks of the Kpelle tribe of central Liberia. A major conclusion for educators is that 'cultural differences in cognition reside more in the situation to which particular cognition processes are applied than in the existence of a process in one cultural group and its absence in another'.)

COMMISSION FOR RACIAL EQUALITY (1974), *In-Service Education of Teachers in Multi-Racial Areas* (London: CRE).

—— (1977), *Urban Deprivation, Racial Inequality and Social Policy* (London: CRE).

—— (1979a), (by M. Anwar), *Ethnic Minorities and the General Election* (London: CRE).

—— (1979b), *A Project on Race Relations* (London: CRE).

—— (1985a), *Ethnic Minorities in Britain: Statistical Information on the Pattern of Settlement* (London: CRE).

—— (1985b), *Positive Action and Equal Opportunity in Employment* (London: CRE).
(These CRE pamphlets provide useful resource material for students' projects examining inequality in the UK. In some cases they are very rich in data and statistics (e.g. 1985a), and in others they are particularly rich in analysis and interpretation (e.g. 1979a).

—— (1987), *Shap Calendar of Religious Festivals* (London: CRE).
(A book full of information on the calendars of many different religions, including Jewish, Hindu, Buddhist, and Sikh, and of religions and philosophies generally. There are many materials and references for the RE teacher.)

CORDOVA, G. (1983) *The Tessellations File* (Diss, Norfolk: Tarquin).
(A booklet for teachers of material for teaching about tessellations, including methods of construction. Photocopiable gridsheets relevant to all the polygonal tessellations are included. An essential resource book for teachers.)

CRITCHLOW, K. (1976), *Islamic Patterns: An Analytical and Cosmological Approach* (London: Thames and Hudson).
(A detailed study of Islamic patterns and their method of construction. The book also provides an introduction to the religious and philosophical background to Islamic art.)

D'AMBROSIO, D. (1985), 'Ethnomathematics and its Place in the History and Pedagogy of Mathematics', *For the Learning of Mathematics*, 5/1: 44–8.
(A highly influential article on the place of ethnomathematics in the classroom. The author is a leading writer on the politics of mathematics teaching.)

DATTA, B. (1932), *The Science of the Sulbas* (Calcutta: Calcutta University Press).
(An exploration of Indian geometry during the Vedic period (i.e. 1000–500 BC) by one of the best-known Indian historians of mathematics. It is now a classic.)

DEPARTMENT OF EDUCATION AND SCIENCE (1982), *Mathematics Counts* (London: HMSO).
(Otherwise known as the 'Cockcroft Report', it was a major government review of school mathematics education in England and Wales.)

——— (1985), *Education for All* (London: HMSO).
(Known as the 'Swann Report', this is a detailed examination of the position and performance of the children of different ethnic minorities in British schools. There is also discussion of the organization and curriculum required to meet the needs of a multicultural society. For more details, see the footnote on p. 5.)

——— (1988), *Mathematics for Ages 5 to 16* (London: HMSO).
(A preliminary National Curriculum document that contains a section on ethnic and cultural diversity which is referred to in Chapter 1.)

——— (1989), *Mathematics in the National Curriculum* (London: HMSO).
(This document sets out a statutory mathematics curriculum for children aged 5–16 in state schools in England and Wales, with effect by stages from 1989. The curriculum is divided into a number of content areas, and individual statements of attainment in these areas are organized hierarchically into a number of levels.)

DHONDY, F. (1978), 'Teach Young Blacks', *Race Today*, 10/4: 80–6.
(An impassioned critique of monocultural and multicultural education and an early advocacy of anti-racist education.)

DILKE, O. A. W. (1987), *Mathematics and Measurement* (London: The British Museum).
(An interesting historical account of Egyptian, Mesopotamian, Greek, and Roman mathematics.)

DYE, D. S. (1981), *The New Book of Chinese Lattice Designs* (New York: Dover).
(A resource book of designs and patterns, taken from the wooden lattices covering traditional Chinese windows.)

EL-SAID, I., and PARMAN, A. (1976), *Geometric Concepts in Islamic Art* (London: World of Islam Festival Publication).

(An account of the methods of construction of many traditional Islamic designs. It includes plates and sources for many patterns from buildings in the Middle East. A useful library reference.)

ERNST, B. (1976), *The Magic Mirror of M. C. Escher* (New York: Ballantyne).

(An introduction to the life and work of Escher. A large number of plates and drawings are included, though there is little guidance on construction compared to Ranucci, listed below.)

ESCHER M. C. (1971), *The Graphic Work of M. C. Escher* (New York: Ballantyne).

(This is more detailed than the previous item and is not restricted to Escher's work. Very helpful for those wishing to draw 'impossible figures'.)

EVES, H. W. (1990), *An Introduction to the History of Mathematics with Cultural Connections* (Philadelphia: Saunders).

(A comprehensive single-volume history from the beginnings of mathematics to modern times. This latest edition increases the converage of non-European mathematics. Of particular interest and value to the mathematics teacher are the extensive runs of problems and miniature projects which conclude each chapter.)

FAUVEL, J., and GRAY, J. (1987), *The History of Mathematics—A Reader* (Basingstoke: Macmillan Education).

(A source book of extracts from original sources or commentaries from early times to Cantor. Contains some material on Babylonian, Egyptian, and Arab mathematics.)

FAUVEL, J. (1990) *Mathematics through History—A Resource Guide* (York: QED Books).

(A useful annotated bibliography, which contains items of interest for multicultural mathematics.)

FLEGG, G. (1983), *Numbers: Their History and Meaning* (Harmondsworth: Penguin).

(This contains many interesting illustrations of counting systems and calculation aids as well as the historical evolution of written numbers and fractions to include irrationals, negative numbers, and complex numbers.)

—— (1989), *Numbers through the Ages* (London: Macmillan).

(An account of the use of numbers in ancient civilizations and in a number of contemporary societies and of the development of methods of calculation and calculating aids.)

FRANZ, M.-L. VON (1978), *Time* (London: Thames and Hudson).

(A useful introduction to differences in cultural concepts of time and of its representation. Rich in cross-curricular ideas.)

FRIBERG, J. (1981), 'Methods and Traditions of Babylonian Mathematics; Plimpton 322, Pythagorean Triples and Babylonian Triangle Parameter Equations', *Historia mathematica*, 8: 277–318.

(A paper on the purpose of the Babylonian tablet, Plimpton 322.)

GALLIAN, J. A. (1990), 'Symmetry in Logos and Hubcaps', *American Mathematical Monthly*, 97/3: 235–8.

(Rather than resort to Hungarian needlework, African, Chinese, Indian, or Arab art for illustrations and examples of symmetry patterns, Joseph Gallian turns to logos in the yellow pages and hubcaps in a car park. While chiding the culturalists, the article nevertheless provides a fine set of references.)

GAY, J., and COLE, M. (1967), *The New Mathematics and an Old Culture* (New York: Holt, Rinehart, and Winston).

(A study of learning and teaching Western mathematics among the Kpelle people of central Liberia. It shows how a traditional culture affects the readiness for learning, indeed the thinking, of children who are being taught concepts for which there are no antecedents in that culture. The mathematical areas considered include arithmetic, geometry, measurement, and logic. A case study in an extreme situation which nevertheless has implications for teachers and schools almost everywhere.)

GERDES, P. (1981), 'Changing Mathematical Education in Mozambique', *Educational Studies in Mathematics*, 12/4: 455–77.

(An interesting comparison between the 'hidden' ideologies of school mathematics of colonial and post-colonial Mozambique.)

—— (1985), 'Conditions and Strategies for Emancipatory Mathematics Education in Underdeveloped Countries', *For the Learning of Mathematics*, 5/1: 15–20.

(An influential justification for ethnomathematics within an African context.)

—— (1988a), 'From Mozambique: Finding the Missing Figures', *Mathematics Teaching*, 124: 18–19.

—— (1988b), 'On Possible Uses of Traditional Angolan Sand Drawings in the Mathematics Classroom', *Educational Studies in Mathematics*, 19/1: 3–22.

(These articles contain 'hidden' geometry in African folk art. They provide examples for classroom investigations.)

GILLINGS, R. J. (1972), *Mathematics in the Time of the Pharaohs* (Cambridge, Mass.: MIT Press).

(A comprehensive and clearly written text on ancient Egyptian mathematics, providing interesting examples for classroom work on numbers, fractions, and geometry.)

GREEN, D. R. (1976a), 'History in Mathematics Teaching: Before the Advent of Modern Mathematics', *Mathematics in School*, 5: 15–17.

—— (1976b), 'History in Mathematics Teaching: Modern Times', *Mathematics in School*, 6: 5–9.

(Two valuable articles surveying the place of the history of mathematics in school teaching, textbooks, examinations, policy documents, and teacher training over the previous hundred years.)

GREVSMÜHL, G. (1988a), 'Mathematics and Modern Art: Module and Structure', *Mathematics Teaching*, 122: 56–61.

—— (1988b), 'Mathematics and Modern Art: Transformation Geometry', *Mathematics Teaching*, 123: 42–6.

(Two of a series of articles on the increased use of mathematics in constructing modern art. Very useful source for developing teaching materials. Could be read directly by older students interested in mathematics and art.)

HALL, H. S., and KNIGHT, S. R. (1897), *Higher Algebra* (London: Macmillan).
(A text for schools and colleges that was popular for half a century.)

HARDY, G. H. (1929), *A Mathematician's Apology* (Cambridge: Cambridge University Press).
(Probably the best-known account of the 'restricted' world view of a pure mathematician. With its clarity, style, and provocative prose, it provides excellent material for discussion in senior classes of the nature and social context of mathematics. A passage from the book is quoted in Chapter 1.)

HARRIS, M. (1988*a*), 'Common Threads', *Mathematics Teaching*, 123: 15–17.

—— (1988*b*), 'Mathematics and Textiles', *Mathematics in School*, 17/4: 24–8.
(An account of an exhibition of textiles ('Common Threads') used to inspire mathematics through pattern.)

HEATH, T. L. (1921), *A History of Greek Mathematics* (2 vols.; Oxford: Oxford University Press).
(The standard two-volume general history of Greek mathematics. Also published by Dover in 1981.)

HEMMINGS, R. (1984), 'Mathematics', in A. Craft and G. Bardell (eds.), *Curriculum Opportunities in a Multi-Cultural Society* (London: Harper and Row), 113–32.
(A chapter containing ideas for linking mathematics and cultures. The topics include Islamic and Rangoli patterns and diverse number and counting systems. Of general interest to mathematics educators.)

HIGHAM, N. J. (1991), 'Solving Linear Equations' in C. Bondi (ed.), *New Applications of Mathematics* (Harmondsworth: Penguin), 33–56.
(This chapter explains why Gaussian elimination remains a popular method for computing solutions of simultaneous linear equations. We refer to this in Chapter 5.)

HOLT, M. (1971), *Mathematics in Art* (Berkshire: Van Nostrand).
(Links are established between mathematics and art, including modern art and architecture, without any exploration of historical or multicultural dimensions.)

HUDSON, B. (1987*a*) *Global Statistics* (York: Centre for Global Education, University of York).
(A resource pack of materials with database software which allows exploration of global statistics. Of interest to social science and mathematics teaching.)

—— (1987*b*), 'Multicultural Mathematics', *Mathematics in School*, 16/4: 34–8.

—— (1990), 'Global Perspectives in the Mathematics Classroom', *Educational Studies in Mathematics*, 21: 129–36.

(An article describing uses of materials in Hudson 1987*a* in developing the theme of inequality. Of interest to teachers.)

IFRAH, G. (1985) *From One to Zero: A Universal History of Number* (New York: Viking).

(A fascinating exploration of the world-wide origins and evolution of numerals and numerical systems. Virtually every system of numeration, simple or advanced, ancient or modern, is here. Copiously illustrated, this survey is an excellent library resource for project work at school level.)

ILEA (1985), *Everyone Counts* (London: ILEA).

(A list of materials and resources for a multicultural approach to school mathematics. Of interest to teachers.)

JOSEPH, G. G. (1984), 'The Multicultural Dimension', *Times Educational Supplement*, Mathematics Extra, 5 Oct.

(This article provides a rationale for a multicultural approach to teaching mathematics.)

—— (1985), 'An Historical Perspective', *Times Educational Supplement*, Mathematics Extra, 11 Oct.

(The importance of history in a multicultural perspective on mathematics is discussed, with an illustration of Vedic multiplication.)

—— (1986), 'A Non-Eurocentric Approach to School Mathematics', *Multicultural Teaching*, 4/2: 30–3.

(A general discussion of the need to counter Eurocentrism in mathematics and a consideration of how this can be achieved in a mathematics classroom.)

—— (1987), 'Foundations of Eurocentrism in Mathematics', *Race and Class*, 28/3: 13–28.

(Different perspectives on the historical development of mathematics and their importance for the mathematics educator. Also reprinted with minor revisions in M. Harris (ed.), *School, Mathematics and Work* (Basingstoke: The Falmer Press, 1991).)

—— (1989), 'Turning the Tables', *Times Educational Supplement*, Mathematics Extra, 5 May.

(An exploration of the 'hidden' geometry behind multiplication tables.)

—— (1990), 'The Politics of Anti-Racist Mathematics', *Multi-Cultural Teaching*, 9/1: 31–3.

(An analysis of how anti-racist multicultural mathematics is perceived by the political and educational establishment in Britain as exemplified in the earlier National Curriculum documents. The article contains a summary of the arguments for such an approach to mathematics.)

—— (1991), *The Crest of the Peacock: Non-European Roots of Mathematics* (London: I. B. Tauris and Co.). Paperback, 1992 (Harmondsworth: Penguin).

(The coverage is world-wide and includes sections on native American and African contributions while providing a detailed examination of Indian, Chinese, and 'Arab' mathematics as well as the mathematics of early civilizations of

Egypt and Mesopotamia. Useful to teachers and accessible for the most part to those who have a school mathematics background.)

JOSEPH, G. G., REDDY, V., and SEARLE-CHATTERJEE, M. (1990), 'Eurocentrism in the Social Sciences', *Race and Class*, 31/4: 1–26.
(An examination of the nature and consequences of the presence of Eurocentrism in three academic disciplines—Economics, Psychology, and Social Anthropology. The article may be of relevance for mathematics teachers who are interested in the philosophical and historical aspects of the emergence of a Eurocentric perspective to knowledge.)

KOJIMA, T. (1954), *The Japanese Abacus* (Rutland, Vt.: Charles E. Tuttle Company).
(An introduction to the history and operation of the modern Japanese abacus.)

KOROS-MIKIS, M., and PANUSKA, R. (1987), 'Pictures with Symmetry and Recursion', *Micromaths*, 3/3: 7–9.
(An article for teachers showing how simple procedures in LOGO reproduce symmetries and recursive patterns.)

KRAUSE, M. C. (1983), *Multicultural Mathematics Material* (Reston, Va.: National Council of Teachers of Mathematics).
(Ideas for classroom activities from different cultures, with very brief background information.)

LANDAU, R., and SWAAN, W. (1967), *Morocco* (London: Elek).
(A book on Moroccan art and culture, of general interest.)

LAWLOR, R. (1982), *Sacred Geometry* (London: Thames and Hudson).
(An attractively illustrated book with design ideas of a multicultural character.)

LAYTON, D. (1973), *Science for the People* (London: George Allen and Unwin).
(A fascinating exploration of the multiple factors that shaped the school science curriculum in England around the middle of the nineteenth century, which saw both the foundations of a state system of mass education and an organized movement for the introduction of science as a school subject.)

LE CORBUSIER (1954), *The Modulor* (London: Faber and Faber).
(The architect, Le Corbusier, describes his 'modulor', the harmonic measuring scale based on a human scale and on mathematical ratios connected to the Fibonacci series and the golden section. Of general interest.)

LIBBRECHT, U. (1973), *Chinese Mathematics in the Thirteenth Century: The Shu-shu Chiu-Chang of Ch'in Chiu-Shao* (Cambridge, Mass.: MIT Press).
(A fascinating, lucid, and scholarly study of a great period of Chinese mathematics.)

LI YAN and DU SHIRAN (1988) *Chinese Mathematics. A Concise History* (Oxford: Oxford University Press).
(A comprehensive history from the earliest to modern times. Besides treating mathematical achievements in a clear and detailed way, the book has valuable chapters on such matters as the evolution of calculations with the abacus, the first (and second) entry of Western mathematics into China, and the revival of

interest in ancient texts. The translators J. N. Crossley and A. W.-C. Lun have also provided four helpful appendices.)

MACGILLAVRY, C. H. (1965), *Symmetry Aspects of M. C. Escher's Periodic Drawings* (Utrecht: A.O. Uitgeversmaatschappij N.V.).
(A book analysing Escher's tessellations by their symmetry groups. Of interest to a mathematician, but makes few concessions to the lay reader.)

M:ATH (1986), *Brochure 61* (Université Paris VII: IREM).
—— (1990), *Brochure 79* (Université Paris VII: IREM).
(Classroom materials with guidance for teachers produced by the M:ATH group (Mathématiques: Approche par des Textes Historiques) based at the IREM, University of Paris VII, 2 Place Jussieu, 75005, Paris. The brochures contain a varied mixture of short units, each unit being associated with a famous mathematician (almost exclusively of Greek or European origin) and an original piece of text. Brochure 61 has sixteen units ranging from Archimedes to von Koch. Brochure 79 has twenty-four units ranging from Euclid to Legendre. Suitable for abler secondary students.)

MATHEMATICAL ASSOCIATION (1988), *Mathematics in a Multicultural Society* (Leicester: Mathematical Association).
(A substantial booklet containing eleven short and varied articles grouped under three headings: Perspectives, Problems, and Practicalities. The concluding section, Sources and Resources, contains over one hundred references.)

—— (1990) *History in the Mathematics Classroom* (Leicester: Mathematical Association).
(A translation of the papers submitted by the French IREM at the 6th International Congress on Mathematical Education (ICME6) at Budapest in 1988. They contain for the most part the materials and reflections of classroom teachers using a historical approach. The ninth and final chapter contains some useful classroom material on Brahmagupta's study of rational quadrilaterals.)

MAXWELL, R. P. (1979), *How to use the Chinese Abacus* (privately published, Phillis Cottage, Holt, Trowbridge, Wilts BA14 6QH).
(A simple and well-written manual on using the abacus to carry out arithmetical operations.)

MELLORS, C. (1978), *The British MP* (Farnborough: Saxon House).
(The book provides statistical information on the characteristics of the House by sex, class, school, etc. A ready reference for data rather than a stimulating read.)

MENNINGER, K. (1969), *Number Words and Number Symbols: A Cultural History of Numbers* (Cambridge, Mass.: MIT Press).
(A leading scholarly text on the subject, though coverage of Africa is inadequate.)

MIDONICK, H. (1968), *The Treasury of Mathematics* (2 vols.; Harmondsworth: Penguin).
(A source book of original texts or commentaries from the Babylonians to Frege and Cantor. Non-European mathematics occupies over two-thirds of the first volume.)

MINISTRY OF EDUCATION (1958), *Teaching Mathematics in Secondary Schools* (Pamphlet 36; London: HMSO).
(A pamphlet more concerned with principles than with methods. The ninth and final chapter is 'The History of Mathematics and its Bearing on Teaching'.)

MMARI, G. R. (1978), 'The United Republic of Tanzania: Mathematics for Social Transformation', in F. J. Swetz (ed.), *Socialist Mathematics Education* (Southampton, Pa.: Burgundy Press), 301–50.
(An article that highlights with interesting examples the inappropriateness of many colonial mathematics texts used in East Africa and how mathematics may be used as an engine for change.)

MOHAMMED BEN MUSA (AL-KHWARIZMI) (1831), *Algebra*, ed. and trans. F. Rosen (Ann Arbor, Mich.: University Microfilm International, 1977).
(Annotated translation of one of the key texts in the early history of mathematics. Short extracts could easily form the basis for teaching materials in schools.)

MOTTERSHEAD, L. (1978), *Sources of Mathematical Discovery* (Oxford: Blackwell).
(Organized thematically in ten sections such as Mathematics in Art, Pastimes, A Hint of Magic, this eclectic resource book provides a large number of starting-points for investigation. Suitable for use at primary and secondary level, it could be used unaided by abler students.)

—— (1985), *Investigations in Mathematics* (Oxford: Blackwell).
(A stimulating collection of ideas for mathematical recreations and investigations based on various cultural or practical starting-points. There are also short biographies of twenty-three mathematicians.)

MULLARD, C. (1985), *Race, Power and Resistance* (London: Routledge and Kegan Paul).
(An influential text laying out the objectives of and rationale for anti-racist education.)

NCTM (1969) *Historical Topics for the Mathematics Classroom*, NCTM (also from QED books, 1 Straylands Grove, York YO3 0EB).
(More a history of school maths topics than a collection of activities for the classroom. Covers numbers and numerals, computation, geometry, trigonometry, algebra and calculus. Each area has an overview and a varied group of short articles.)

NEEDHAM, J. (1959), *Science and Civilisation in China* (Cambridge: Cambridge University Press), iii.
(Besides the section on mathematics, this volume contains valuable material on astronomy and map-making. A short history is followed by a detailed thematic discussion of mathematical achievements. It concludes with a comparison between the decline of mathematics in China and the development of Western mathematics in Renaissance Europe.)

—— (1973), 'The Historian of Science as Ecumenical Man', in S. Nakayama and N. Sivin (eds.), *Chinese Science* (Cambridge, Mass.: MIT Press), 1–8.

(A collection of articles about the history of Chinese science and at the same time a tribute to Joseph Needham's contribution as a historian of Chinese science.)

NELSON, R. D. (1977a), 'Mathematical Models in the Classroom', *Mathematical Gazette*, 416: 82–92.

(One of the illustrative examples involves the collection, analysis, and comparison of rank-population data for the cities and towns of thirteen countries.)

—— (1977b), 'A Regular Pentagon Construction', *Mathematical Gazette*, 417: 215–16.

(An example of classroom mathematics emanating from a cultural artefact—an Indian *yantra*, the *sri chakra*.)

NEUGEBAUER, O. (1962), *The Exact Sciences in Antiquity* (New York: Harper).

(One of the great classics in the history of mathematics. The clarity and perceptiveness of the author is best seen in the manner in which he assesses the contribution of Ancient Egypt and Babylonia to mathematics and astronomy.)

NEWNHAM (1986), *Employment, Unemployment and Black People* (London: Runnymede Trust).

(A reference guide for students engaged on project work on inequality.)

NISSEN, P. (1988), 'Sand-drawing of Vanuatu', in *Mathematics in a Multicultural Society* (Leicester: Mathematical Association), 34–7.

(See above, Mathematical Association.)

NKETIA, J. H. KWABENA (1974), *The Music of Africa* (London: Gollancz).

(Designed by a leading scholar as an introduction for the general reader and student. The twelfth chapter, 'The Rhythmic Basis of Instrumental Music', begins to reveal some of the numerical complexities of African drumming.)

OFFICE OF POPULATION CENSUSES AND SURVEYS (1987–9), *Labour Force Survey 1985, 1986, 1987* (London: HMSO).

(An annual reference source for statistics on labour, employment, and unemployment, of interest to social science projects. Also a source used in the discussion of the UK population in the 'Percentage' section of Chapter 3.)

O'HANIAN, H. C. (1985), *Physics* (New York: Norton), i.

(An undergraduate text, including a case study of symmetry and tessellation in physics.)

OPEN UNIVERSITY (1976), *Written Numbers* (AM 289N3; Milton Keynes: Open University Press).

(A useful and well-illustrated source of material on the development of numerals.)

OUCHI, H. (1978), *Japanese Optical and Geometrical Art* (New York: Dover).

(A fascinating resource of 170 pages of optical designs for use in art and design.)

POLYA, G. (1965), *Mathematical Discovery* (New York: Wiley), ii.

(One of the books in which this distinguished mathematician developed further the ideas about heuristics in mathematical problem-solving which were first proposed in his 1945 classic *How to Solve It*.)

POPP, W. (1978), *History of Mathematics: Topics for Schools* (Milton Keynes: Open University Press).

(A comprehensive collection of topics from history which could be used by teachers as the basis for classroom materials.)

POTTS, R. (1845), *Elements of Geometry* (Cambridge: Cambridge University Press).

—— (1876), *Elementary Arithmetic, with Brief Notices of its History* (Cambridge: Cambridge University Press).

—— (1879), *Elementary Algebra* (London: Longman).

(Three nineteenth-century school textbooks that incorporated historical material.)

PURCE, J. (1974), *The Mystic Spiral* (London: Thames and Hudson).

(A fascinating account of the cultural and mathematical dimensions of the spiral.)

RÅDE, L., and NELSON, R. D. (1984), *Adventures with your Computer* (Harmondsworth: Penguin).

(Adventures 4 and 13 give the necessary background for the computer simulations of dice games in the 'Statistical Ideas' section of Chapter 3.)

RANUCCI, E. R., and TEETERS, J. L. (1977) *Creating Escher Type Drawings* (Palo-Alto, Calif.: Creative Publishing).

(This is a thorough introduction to creating Escher patterns through transformation geometry, of general interest as well as of interest to teachers.)

RESNIKOFF, H. L. and WELLS, R. O. (1984), *Mathematics and Civilization* (New York: Dover).

(A model of how mathematics and culture can be combined to produce interesting mathematical activities for senior school and college students. Its major drawback is its strong Eurocentric bias.)

RIBERA, J. (1970), *Music in Ancient Arabia and Spain* (New York: Da Capo Press).

(The eleventh and sixteenth chapters discuss the five classic Arab rhythms: *hezej*, first *takil*, second *takil*, *makhuri*, and *ramel*, and offer scope for elementary work with fractions. The appendix offers forty-three *cantigas*: thirteenth-century Spanish melodies each in one of these rhythms.)

ROSS, A. (1984), *The Story of Mathematics* (London: Black).

(A book written for children which provides mainly historical information on mathematics from different cultures—the non-European elements could be augmented.)

ROTA, GIAN-CARLO (1986), 'Mathematics and its History', and 'Misreading the History of Mathematics', in M. Kac, G.-C. Rota, and J. T. Schwartz, *Discrete Thoughts* (Boston, Mass.: Birkhauser), 157–61, 231–4.

(Two pithy and stimulating reviews in a miscellany of twenty-six articles on subjects such as 'Artificial Intelligence' (Schwartz), 'Doing Away with Science' (Kac), and 'Combinatorics' (Rota).)

RUPERT, W. W. (1900–1), *Famous Geometrical Theorems and Problems* (issued in four parts; Boston, Mass.: D. C. Heath).

220 Bibliography

(An example of a school textbook which uses history to enhance and enliven presentation.)

SCHOOLS COUNCIL PROJECT (1980), *Statistics in your World* (Slough: Foulsham).

(A dated but well-presented compendium of statistics for classroom use.)

SEIDENBERG, A. (1960), 'The Diffusion of Counting Practices', *University of California Publications in Mathematics*, 3/4: 215–99.

—— (1962), 'The Ritual Origins of Counting', *Archives for History of Exact Sciences*, 2: 1–40.

(Two papers which explore the hypothesis that every one of the known counting systems was invented just once in one geographical location and then spread to other places.)

SIVARD, R. L. (1987), *World Military and Social Expenditures, 1987/8* (Washington, DC: World Priorities).

(A compilation of statistics on military and social expenditures, including interesting graphic presentations. Useful for projects in schools in social science or mathematics. Also of general interest.)

SMITH, D. E. (1923–5), *History of Mathematics* (2 vols.; Boston, Mass.: Ginn).

(The first volume is a history of elementary mathematics on chronological and regional lines. The second volume treats the subject thematically, the sections being number, geometry, algebra, trigonometry, and calculus.)

—— and MIKAMI, Y. (1914), *A History of Japanese Mathematics* (Chicago: Open Court Publishing Company).

(A short history which also contains information on Chinese and Korean mathematics.)

SORRELL, N., and NARAYAN, R. (1980), *Indian Music in Performance: A Practical Introduction* (Manchester: Manchester University Press).

(Principally a study of the *sarangi*, the original Indian bowed stringed instrument, of which Ram Narayan is a leading exponent. The section on 'Practice' has intersections with mathematics. For example, there is a discussion of the 24 permutations on a 4-note *palta* or the partitioning of a 32-note phrase in various ways by bowing. The section on rhythmic structure, *rag* with *tal*, offers further possibilities for numerical work.)

STERN, M. D., and NEJAD, L. A. M (1991), 'Conflict between Religious and National Traditions in Iran: A Group Case Study', *Teaching Mathematics and its Applications*, 10/3: 113–15.

(A short paper discussing the conflicting demands on those observing both the Persian and Muslim calendars. It includes an algorithm for converting from Muslim to Gregorian dates.)

STEVENS, P. S. (1981), *Handbook of Regular Patterns* (Cambridge, Mass.: MIT Press).

(A 400-page anthology of regular plane patterns. Conceived as a handbook for artists and designers, it contains numerous examples of structurally similar patterns from different cultures and historical periods. The four sections are titled 'symmetric groups', 'point groups', 'the seven line groups' (freize patterns), and 'the seventeen plane groups' (wallpaper patterns).)

STONE, M. (1981), *The Education of Black Children in Britain: The Myth of Multicultural Education* (London: Fontana).
(An influential critique of multicultural education.)

STRUIK, D. J. (1963), 'On Ancient Chinese Mathematics', *Mathematics Teacher*, 56: 424–32.
(An excellent introductory article for teachers.)

SWANN REPORT: *see* Department of Education and Science (1985).

SWETZ, F. J. (1972), 'The Amazing Chiu Chang Suan Shu', *Mathematics Teacher*, 65: 423–30.
(A good introduction for teachers to the classic text of early Chinese mathematics.)

—— (1986), 'The History of Mathematics as a Source of Classroom Problems', *School Science and Mathematics*, 86/1: 33–8.

—— (1989), 'Using Problems from the History of Mathematics in the Classroom', *Mathematics Teacher*, 82: 370–7.
(Two articles encouraging teachers to use problems with a cultural or historical or social perspective. Swetz argues that they can impart a sense of the continuity of mathematical development, illustrate changes in solution processes, and provide historical, social, or cultural insights.)

—— and KAO, T. I. (1977), *Was Pythagoras Chinese? An Examination of Right Triangle Theory in Ancient China* (Pennsylvania State University Press).
(This striking title belongs to a book which provides a clear and scholarly study of right-triangle theory contained in the Chinese classic, *Chiu Chang Suan Shu*. In it appears the famous broken bamboo, the taut rope, and other 'Pythagorean' problems which are found in a number of cultures. Will be of interest to senior classes at all levels.)

THOM, A. (1967), *Megalithic Sites in Britain* (Oxford: Oxford University Press).
(A book based on the results of surveys of Megalithic circles, alignments, and standing stones. Thom proposes that these are consistent with a single unit of measurement, the Megalithic yard of 2.72 feet, and speculates on the geometric design of the circles and rings. He suggests nearly all the elliptical rings are based on triangles which are almost Pythagorean.)

THOM, R. (1973) 'Modern Mathematics: Does it Exist?', in A. G. Howson (ed.), *Developments in Mathematical Education* (Cambridge: Cambridge University Press), 194–209.
(Text of a paper given at the 2nd International Congress on Mathematical Education (ICME) at Exeter in 1972.)

TUFTE, E. (1983), *The Visual Display of Quantitative Information* (Cheshire, Conn.: Graphics Press).
(The source for some illustrations in Chapter 3. A beautifully produced, copi-

ously illustrated, 'celebration of data graphics', notable for its historical and geographical range and for its search for definitions of 'graphical integrity and excellence'.)

TYTHERLEIGH, B., and WATSON, A. (1987), 'Mathematics and Dance', *Mathematics Teaching*, 121: 39–43.
(An article for teachers about the use of dance in teaching mathematics and pattern to primary-school children.)

UNESCO (1989), *Mathematics, Education, and Society*, ed. C. Keitel, P. Damerow, A. Bishop, and P. Gerdes (Science and Technology Education, Document Series No. 35; Paris: UNESCO).
(Reports and papers presented in the Fifth Day Special Programme of the 6th International Conference on Mathematical Education (ICME6) at Budapest in 1988 organized around four fields: Mathematics Education and Culture; Society and Institutionalized Mathematics Education; Education Institutions and the Individual Learner; and Mathematics Education in the Global Village.)

UNICEF (1988), *The State of the World's Children* (Oxford: Oxford University Press).
(Annual reports on infant health and mortality, including grim graphs and statistics. A useful library reference and teaching resource.)

WADE, D. (1982), *Geometric Patterns and Borders* (London: Wildwood House).
(A collection of hundreds of patterns and designs from around the world. Useful for art and design and of mathematical interest.)

WAERDEN, VAN DER (1983), *Geometry and Algebra in Ancient Civilisations* (Berlin: Springer Verlag).
(Materials from Babylonian, Egyptian, Indian, Greek, Arab, Chinese, and Megalithic sources are interwoven in seven sections: Pythagorean triangles; Chinese and Babylonian mathematics; Greek algebra; Diophantos and his Predecessors; Diophantine Equations; Popular Mathematics; and Liu Hui and Aryabhata. It is argued that these mathematical developments emanated from an earlier mathematical tradition located, possibly, in neolithic Europe.)

WILKINSON, A. (1985), *It's Not Fair* (London: Christian Aid, British Council of Churches).
(A source of ideas for teaching about inequality designed to raise political awareness.)

WILTSHIRE, A. (1983), *The Geometrics File* (Diss, Norfolk: Tarquin).
(A teachers' resource book about tessellation and shapes with practical ideas for recreation and investigation.)

WHITE, N., RIDING, M., and NOCK, D. (1987), *Mathematics for All* (Trowbridge, Wilts.: Wiltshire Education Authority).
(A useful collection of multicultural materials for use with infant, junior, and lower secondary classes. The topics include number systems, Vedic squares, networks, multiplication methods, mirror work, 'squares' (a theme incorporating Islamic patterns, magic squares, tangrams and tilings), and games from around the world.)

WORLD BANK (1981), *World Development Report 1981* (New York: Oxford University Press).

(A useful source of data, including Table 7.6 of our Chapter 7.)

YOUNG, S. (1864), *Practical Arithmetic* (Derby: J. & C. Mozley).

(The title-page reads: 'A system of Practical Arithmetic, adapted to the use of schools; containing the Fundamental Rules, and their application to Mercantile, Cotton Spinning, Manufacturing and Mechanical Calculations. Also comprehending numerous rules and examples in the various departments of Cotton Spinning, Mechanics etc., useful to Cotton Spinners, Millwrights, Engineers and Artizans in general. Containing much more information upon those subjects than has ever before been published in any treatise on arithmetic.')

ZASLAVSKY, C. (1973), *Africa Counts* (Boston, Mass.: Prindle, Weber and Schmidt). Paperback, 1979 (New York: Lawrence Hill Books).

(A widely known text showing examples of African mathematics, notably in topics such as numbers, measures, games, geometry, and design. The coverage has both a historical perspective as well as a regional dimension.)

Index